EVERY STEP OF THE WAY

By

John Hammersley

John Hammersley is a retired Anglican priest, who was once Executive Secretary of Parish and People He is glad to acknowledge his debt to Bishop Henry de Candole, one of the founders and President of P & P, who probably first developed his enthusiasm for church liturgy.

Acknowledgements to many people whom I have quoted unwittingly. I hope deliberate quotations are all acknowledged in the text.

So far as the "psalms" are concerned, Parish & People will be only too pleased if you wish to photocopy and use these, either for private prayers or in public. We should appreciate an acknowledgement of the source.

You can find more modern "psalms" on the website, www.psalmsoflife.com

ISBN: 1 873529 72 4
© Parish and People
The Old Mill, Spetisbury, Blandford Forum, Dorset DT11 9DF

Printed by Stantonbury Parish Print
6 Stable Yard, Downs Barn, Milton Keynes MK14 7RZ. 01908 609214

CONTENTS

Foreword

PART ONE

PART TWO

PART THREE

Foreword

by the Rt Revd Dr John Saxbee, Bishop of Lincoln

"Parish & People" was famous in the 1950s for having changed church notice boards in England. Before then, the main Sunday service had usually been Matins, either said or more often sung, but it now became the "Parish Communion." It was all part of the Liturgical Movement, which P & P helped to introduce to Britain from France. There was also a growing interest in the seasons of the church year. So "Every Step of the Way" fits into the story of liturgical work done by previous generations of Anglicans.

John Hammersley began writing "psalms" in the late 1980s, aware that this was a way of praying which could be used by modern people too, as much as by King David. David Adam had started to use Celtic forms for modern prayers, so why should we not use a form of poetry in English, as it is used in Hebrew prayer? He wrote a "psalm" to celebrate the millennium, which was used in public worship in the year 2000. It can be found in the other book of psalms published by P & P, "Psalms for the Synod" as well as on his Psalms of Life website.

In addition to his Psalm for each season of the Church's year, John provides a homily which explains the main emphasis of the season and often sheds new light on familiar themes.

"Every Step of the Way" will be an encouragement to us all not only to continue to pray, but to use the stepping stones of the liturgical year as a help in following the Way.

Every Step of the Way

EVERY STEP OF THE WAY

PART ONE

ONE

INTRODUCTION

"The calendar ... tells the story of the saving work of Christ in such a way that Christian people today may be helped in their spiritual life and their discipleship."
(Church of England Liturgical Commission 1997)

Life depends on breathing in and breathing out. In the same way, the Christian year has two halves. First, from Advent to Pentecost, is like breathing in the stories of the Christian tradition (made up of the birth, life, death and resurrection of Jesus Christ, preceded by Advent and concluded with Pentecost). The second half of the year is made up of Trinity Sunday and the weeks "after Trinity," concluding with the Kingdom Season in preparation for Advent again, like breathing out the stories of faith.

In the same sort of way this selection of stories and psalms provides a breathing-in of some of the images of the season, followed by a breathing-out of the ideas in a psalm of prayer or worship.

Religion, like family life, has a way of ordering a regular round of celebrations that give a pattern and make some kind of sense of the whole year. As we go round the year's celebrations, we gain some sort of perspective of time'– past, present and future. One of the advantages of living in a Vicarage is that the pattern of the year becomes imprinted on your soul, or at least your unconscious mind. It is an advantage fewer people may be able to share. That is a loss, to us as individuals, and to our society.

For it is at present fashionable to reject religion. God is dead, after all, isn't he? And yet there's always a bit of a niggle. There are all those questions about life and death that we still have to deal with somehow. We look for a framework, a non-religious framework for living by. But what we mean when we say that, is that we are looking for a "non sectarian" framework, because any framework is, strictly speaking, a religious one. For any framework, however vague, has to be

7

able to deal with our questions, not just at times of crisis, but every step of the way. One of our problems with religion is that we want to reject the guidance that is provided for us in a restricted ("religious") way, on Sundays, or Fridays, or at specific times of prayer, only. Many people say they don't have a problem about God, just the church. Specifically, many of us have problems about the "fairies at the bottom of the garden" kind of religion, which is seen to be expecting us to believe things no sane person would ever countenance. That kind of religion we sometimes call "fundamentalist" and it can lead to terrible madness, including the Hamas style of suicide bombing and the events of September 11th 2001 at the World Trade Centre in New York. The question we struggle with is whether there is any truth behind all the impossible stories, whether there is a Way. That is why following the seasons of the year might provide a different kind of framework that allows us to follow, in this case, the Christian stories without having to believe them without question. The first Christians were said to be followers of "The Way."

For our own health, it may be that we need to recover the pattern of breathing again.

PSALM

1. It's comforting to think again over the past:
   for memories needn't be threatening.

2. I look back with easy detachment:
   as you, God, look on me in your infinite mercy.

3. Earlier battles have faded, they're not so critical:
   past stupidities no longer have power;

4. previous glories have a mellower radiance:
   recalling former happiness can staunch my depression.

5. So, God, increase my faith:
   help us, Father, to worship you in everything
   that's happened,

6. strengthen and confirm our trust in you:
   grant us to share the vision of your faithfulness.

7. The future holds fearful uncertainties:
   the struggle ahead looks long and painful.

8. The gap between rich and poor seems set to widen;
   conflicts of races and cultures to escalate into violence;

9. we continually misuse our environment:
    yet your purposes are ever closer to fruition.

10. The end of our exploring is to arrive where we began:
    and know ourselves better than before.

11. So, God, deepen my hope:
    help us, Christ our Lord, to face the future with
    your obedience,

12. for all things shall be well:
    all manner of things shall be well.

13. God, you are eternally now:
    all time is focused in this present moment.

14. Even when I've been through a time like this before:
    I need to approach it fresh and with humbler reverence.

15. Help me travel on, adoring your love:
    to go forward, serving the world around me,

16. and to see these are not two separate journeys:
    but roads that meet in this moment in your presence.

17. So, God, widen my love:
    help us, Holy Spirit, to be conscious of your
    sustaining power,

18. for this time is given us out of your grace:
    we'll find your eternal present within our
    own experiences.

THE JOURNEY

It was the idiosyncratic philosopher, Alan Watts, who first made me feel enthusiastic about the rhythm of the festivals of the year (Myth & Ritual in Christianity: Alan W Watts: Thames & Hudson. 1954). It is their very repetition that makes them so powerful, to become part of our way of thinking. Each year, as we go round the same familiar rhythm of thoughts and stories, we are able (if we wish) to enter more fully or at a deeper level into the pattern. To use another metaphor, it is like going on the same journey time after time. Sometimes, that can be just ... well, boring. But, sometimes, it can make you notice things you had not seen before. It can be very exciting indeed.

Worship can be a similar sort of journey. Dag Hammarsjold's phrase that "the longest journey is the journey inwards" is using the same image about the spiritual journey. For faith is not just a reverent and careful remembering of a past history; but the recurrent re-living of what is timeless truth, year by year. Alan Watts makes the connection between the rhythm of the day, the monastic hours, the seasons of the year and the pattern of Christian festivals.

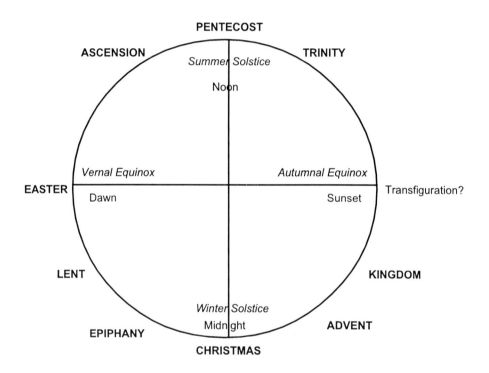

Drawing based on Alan Watts in *Myth and Ritual in Christianity* (1954)

Of course, it is quite possible to work with a different pattern. Each major world faith has its own slightly different rhythm around the circle of the year, though many of the same ideas recur, Or it is possible to make up your own quite different pattern. Jostein Gaarder does that in *The Solitaire Mystery*, where there is a year for playing cards. As there are 52 weeks, each week belongs to one playing card – but 7 x 52 = 364, so there has to be another day for the joker (and two joker days every four years!). As there are four seasons of the year, these are the four suits, so the year begins with 13 weeks of the diamonds in the spring; then the summer is for clubs; hearts for autumn; and spades for winter. That is one pattern, but there is also another one, for the year is also divided into 13 months of 28 days (which also makes up 364 days), one month for each denomination of card in a suit.

> The first month is Ace and the last month is King. Then there is an interval of four years between every two Joker Days. It begins with the year of the diamonds, followed by the year of the clubs, then hearts and finally spades. In this way all the cards have their own week and month.

Such a pattern, in the story, makes the magic island of the playing cards have special rhythms all of its own, which fits well for a population of cards, including a joker.

> 'So what week are we in now?'
> 'Yesterday was the last day in the King of Spades's week, but it was also the last day in the King of Spades's month ... today is Joker Day - or the first of two Joker Days. It will be celebrated with a big banquet.'
> (Gaarder, *The Solitaire Mystery*: Phoenix House, London. 1997 p194)

For some people, the patterns and rhythms of faith nowadays seem to be alien, even foreign, as strange as the year of playing cards. Yet we all create our own patterns, if we are not provided with one. And perhaps in any case we can all benefit from the occasional "big banquet" to celebrate. Even if (perhaps especially if) there is nothing particular to celebrate. We may make the excuse of an "un-birthday" party or find another reason if we cannot use the festivals that are around us. Our present holidays originated, of course, in the annual holy days that used to provide just such a journey for us.

I was at a weekend conference once, at which a small group of men and women had been exploring together our common faith and its relevance to our daily lives and work. We had particularly shared some very painful personal agonies, which a few of the participants had begun, tentatively, to describe openly to the others. It was late at night, and we were tired and a little battered by the experience, which was quite new to all of us. The night outside was dark through the big windows of the old house by the seaside. But, in the corner of the room where we were meeting was a pool of light from the two big standard lamps, either side of the fireplace. It seemed as if we were sharing a warming light, despite the darkness of the world beyond. It felt that there was comfort in the support of the other members of the group, while the real world to which we each had to return separately the following day was threatening and negative. Perhaps it would be better to stay here, in the comforting warmth, rather than to start to think about going back to our normal life again.

Then someone noticed through the gloom outside the window, as he was feeling depressed and staring ahead, that there was a lighthouse beacon shining its light across the sea, clear and bright, beckoning. Perhaps, after all, God was "out there" too, ready to show us the way we could go and the journey we could follow?

PSALM

1. At the start, it's only the journey that matters:
      just to be on the move creates the excitement;

2. I need to keep moving to be making progress:
      dreams and possibilities make the travelling
      worth while.

3. But an older person wants things to remain as they were:
      an ancient culture strives to conserve the status quo,

4. for looking back stirs memories of glory:
      history's more exciting than the threat
      of something new.

5. On the journey inwards it's God who moves us forward:
      tradition can give me the start that I need,

6. for you are the journey we travel:
      you are the goal to which I aspire.

7. Later, it's novelty that motivates us:
      each day there must be something different;

8. every step brings the chance of a new experience:
      round the corner is something
      I've never seen before.

9. But an older person likes to return to well-known places:
      there's comfort in seeing the same people over again;

10. a relationship depends on repeating successful outings:
      to be together is more interesting than doing
      something fresh.

11. On the journey inwards you too have walked my path:
    you bring from your treasures things old and new;

12. your presence sustains me in all I have to face:
    you are in us now, as once you were with your
    friends on earth.

13. Finally to complete the journey is our primary aim:
    to have finished what we had decided to do -

14. never mind the way we go:
    stopping and taking notice will only delay.

15. But an older person needs to take a rest:
    to stop and stare is central to any pilgrimage;

16. what is life if there's no time for contemplation:
    we need strength to continue and space to
    consider where we are.

17. On the journey inwards, I need time to reach beyond time:
    give us your spirit and power to continue
    faithful to the end,

18. for the last may be the hardest part
    I need your strength and hope for the final ascent.

JOURNEYS MEAN WAITING

I don't think St Paul was a very good teacher! He had a sudden conversion in a flash of inspiration on the way to Damascus, and he didn't have to struggle through all the agonies that most other believers have had to do. First of all, he expected everyone else to be a strenuous Pharisee. After his conversion, he expected everyone else to be a strenuous Christian. He was very hard, for example, on John Mark, who came for part of the journey, but then wanted to give up. Paul was a fanatic; he could see things quite clearly for himself, black and white.

My daughter was trying to do some homework, but she said she couldn't understand it. Would I help her? Well, yes, I could see exactly what she had to do, but she couldn't understand. I did not find it easy to help her. She had to struggle through it all herself. I remember having a similar experience with teaching children. One of my colleagues said he had always been hopeless at maths. But he was a good teacher; he understood the problems other people experienced. All I could do was to wait until the penny had dropped, and not be much use in helping it on its way.

Every Step of the Way

But there is one thing about St Paul. He went on journeys, the great missionary journeys we were supposed to learn about at school. Maybe his journeys are a better way to think of learning. You need to struggle at a problem before you really understand it. You need to fight your way round the world before you can fully grasp what it's really like.

Many people think Christian faith comes like it came to Saul - in a blinding flash, at about the time of confirmation, or at some change or crisis in life. Well, it may. But you may not be a very good teacher of faith, if that's how it came to you. For most of us, faith comes only through the struggle of the journey. Right up to the end of our life, we shall not actually arrive at the finishing line (death is the finishing line). The struggle and the waiting may make us better teachers. But we shall not achieve all we would like. We never pass the test; Christians are always learners, wearing 'L' plates. Our faith licences are only provisional. But then, that's what you would expect of people who are called to be disciples, learners. Part of the struggling through the journey may be simply a matter of waiting. Bird watchers sometimes say that you have to spend a long time just looking at a place, before you can see anything at all. Nevertheless, at times, the landscape seems to change somehow, and you may be able to see all sorts of things, including the birds you have come to see. The waiting is not just waiting in boredom, but part of the struggle to see.

Someone once said it is a sign of old age if you have not recently discarded a major opinion, or acquired a new one.

PSALM

1. At the bus stop you can notice a person's faith:
   for it's faith that can help me stand and
   wait with patience.

2. The advert said credit would take the waiting out of wanting:
   but to take away the waiting is to miss the excitement.

3. Whenever I have to wait, God teach me to wait on you:
   to expect your purposes to be fulfilled
   in eager anticipation,

4. for you never act without thought or care:
   to you all time is eternity,
   your patience is never exhausted.

5. I will wait on God, and you will not let me down:
   I shall keep still and listen for the sounds of silence;

6. you speak peace to me when I'm open to your stillness:
   as I begin to relax you fill me with your total security.

7. I will wait on you, my God, at a time of quiet:
   my activity itself can be an offering to you.

8. In the thick of things, I'll find a space for reflection:
   to recall your presence is a prayer,
   like an arrow shot into the sky.

9. I'm ready and waiting on you now:
   as I wait here, you increase my faith in you.

10. We wait for your love and your goodness to be shown to us:
    as we share this expectancy,
    you strengthen our life together.

(Published in "Psalms for the Synod" by Parish & People)

EVERY STEP OF THE WAY

PART TWO

TWO

THE ANTE-ROOM

ADVENT – the coming time.

> *The beginning of the Christian year is a preparation for the festival of the birth of Christ (Christ-mas), just as there is a season of preparation before the other great feast of Easter. Advent means the coming time, the arrival.*

It was the beginning of an Advent sermon, in the year when we were all being encouraged to buy shares in the newly privatised "British Gas" company. We had to remember the telephone number to register our interest in buying some shares (0272 272 272). And the adverts were all about looking for the one person who hadn't heard the message, Sid, and telling him about it. So the sermon began: "Advent means coming. Christ is coming. If you see Sid, tell him!" For there is a missionary slant to Advent. It is not for nothing that St Andrew's day (traditionally the first missionary, because he brought his brother Peter to meet Jesus) is on the last day of November. Perhaps it is because Advent has a strong message:

> Now is the time to awake out of sleep; for our salvation is nearer now than when we first believed. (Romans 13.11)

There was a time when preachers thought they always had to produce a strong message, hell-fire and thunderbolts, and do their best to frighten us all into listening. During the 1950s there was a post-world-war-two mission to London, and many of the preachers were strongly evangelical, determined to get the message across to a waiting and expectant public. So the mission was called the "Christian Commando Campaign." I remember one preaching service. The sermon began with a text from the ending of the Bible, the book of the Revelation to John: "Behold, I stand at the door … and knock." It was spoken very quietly, and slowly, several times. There was a pause. Suddenly the preacher banged on the pulpit with his fist. Several people around me jumped. And he shouted at the top of his voice, "Can you hear him knocking?" The sermon went on with such histrionics for what seemed like hours, and was probably about 35 minutes. After a while, it seemed to me to be very boring. Obviously, the preacher felt he had a strong message to get across, and needed to shock us into listening.

The message of Advent is clear enough, then. Awake out of sleep, for you never know when God may call you and expect you to be ready. Portents may appear at any time, the signs of the breaking in of a new age (or it may be the end of the world), suddenly, like a thief in the night, unexpected. It is a message reinforced by stories of the "near miss" of asteroids that come near to colliding with the earth. But, in case you worry about it, they say such a "near miss" happens quite frequently. If you imagine it like a darts board with the bulls eye as the earth, and the moon orbiting around the doubles at the edge, such a "near miss" asteroid would be well beyond the surrounds of the darts board anyway. Nevertheless, it tends to jolt us out of our usual complacency! So wake out of your sleep. John Donne was making a similar point in a sermon at St Paul's Cathedral in London on Easter Day 1619:

> All our life is but a going out to the place of execution, to death. Now was any man seen to sleep in the cart between Newgate and Tyburn? Between the prison and the place of execution does any man sleep? And we sleep all the way; from the womb to the grave we are never thoroughly awake...

It's the message of Advent. Because "our salvation is nearer than when we first believed." They are words I associate with Advent; they give me a warm feeling of Christmas coming. But do they mean that we are on the way to our death, so we had better watch out and concentrate? Or do they mean that the end of the world is at hand, and we had all better prepare for it?

If it's about the coming of the end of everything, St Paul was just wrong. Just as in the Mark, Matthew and Luke Gospels where "the present generation will live to see it all." The idea was that Jesus was going to return and save his chosen disciples, and there would be signs and portents to point to it all. We are certainly more and more aware of the portents. "Nations will stand helpless," says Luke – just as the United Nations seems to do over the latest crisis in the Middle East or Africa.–"The roar and surge of the sea"– just as global warming, in the months at the ending of the year especially, make us aware that only a few centimetres need to be added to the sea levels and parts of our planet will disappear beneath the waves. "Terror at the thought of what is coming"– certainly we are more conscious of terror-ism, and of the fear of crime that seems endemic to our world, these days. "The celestial powers will be shaken"– it may be a meteor collision, blocking out the sun, such as may have happened to extinguish the dinosaurs. There is plenty to make us aware of the eschatological warnings, of the last days, of the end of the world! Then, say the Gospel stories, the Son of Man will come...

The Second Coming of Christ is not a popular doctrine, in our day. Especially if it means we have to face all these horrors, ourselves, first. What if the end of our world is near and not just several billion years away when the sun runs out of steam? I suppose every generation reads these words and has to think: "it could be you!" But, after 65 generations, it's easier to feel that it can't possibly be us. And yet... Advent does make you think. In any case, one thing most certainly will happen to us'– we all of us do have to die, sooner or later.

The Luke Gospel adds a message of hope. When you see all this, stand up and hold your heads up high. It is not something to be depressed about, but to rejoice and look forward to. Can you trust God enough to do that? For the Advent message is a message of hope in God, not of doom and destruction. It reminds me of the feeling I get in a jumbo jet. They start by terrifying you, explaining how to put on life jackets and get out of the plane by jumping onto a raft. Then they point out what to do if the lights fail, or there isn't any oxygen. Then the Captain tells you to fasten your seat belt because we're experiencing a little turbulence at the moment. And you notice the wing is juddering a bit. What are you supposed to do? Are we going to crash? The trouble is you can't do anything about it. All you can do, and it is a lot, is to trust the Captain.

PSALM

1. I look out from afar and see the power of God:
   there's a cloud that's coming to cover the earth.

2. Go out to meet him and say:
   "Are you the one who is coming as
   king of your people?"

3. High and low, rich and poor, go out to meet him:
   sisters and brothers, go to him and say,

4. "Listen, you who lead your people like sheep:
   are you the shepherd who's coming to guide us?

5. "Be ready to help us, we need strong leaders:
   come and be king of your faithful people.

6. "Rise up in your might and judge the earth:
   bring everyone under your justice, but rule us gently."

7.   For we stand at the verge of a new horizon:
           yet lack the will to take hold of your future.

8.   I look out from afar:
           and I see the power of God that's coming;

9.   go out to meet him and say:
           "Tell us, are you the one who's coming
           as king of your people?"

ADVENT – time for preparing.

Advent means what is coming, and we're not very good at what's coming to us. We like to go to a modern "Gypsy Smith" or Russell Grant to learn what the future might hold for us. The first bit of the newspaper most of us read is our "stars." Some Christian believers have a problem with such horoscopes, because they are pagan. They shouldn't have. Part of the Christmas story is about "wise men from the east," the "magoi," followers of horoscopes in the stars. But is this appropriate today, apart from having a bit of a laugh at how banal and generalised the predictions usually are? Is it a proper way to prepare for what is coming?

I was at a funeral at the local Crematorium, and found myself saying to people there that we all of us feel a bit wobbly inside when we come to someone's funeral, no matter how much we may have been expecting it. Why is that? Because, of course, it is a reminder of our mortality, since we all have to die sometime. But also because looking into the future is always a bit scary, and surprisingly, being reminded of someone else's life and remembering their past, also makes us aware of what still might be in store for us. When someone from the previous generation of your own family dies, and especially if that leaves me as the 'head' of the family, there's an odd feeling like that of standing on the edge of a precipice. It's up to me now to be at the leading edge; what is going to happen, now?

We have just been keeping the four Sundays of the Kingdom, the run-up to Advent. There was a time when Advent was supposed to copy Lent, a preparation for the great Christian festival, and so it was meant to last for six weeks, another forty days like Lent. In the liturgical revisions of the 20th century there was provision for a nine-week preparation for Christmas. The Kingdom season is modelled on a more ancient tradition that fits in with our modern season of remembrance. We have "remembered" the past, the saints and the departed. November is a bit of a month for death and dying. Remembrance may be nostalgic sometimes; it sure does something to your inside, too.

In 2000, I came back from a holiday in South Africa. That felt to me a bit the same. I have lived with the "problem" of South Africa most of my life. And now it is coming out of the depths of inhumanity and looking forward to the future in freedom. But it isn't quite as simple as that! Black students at Fort Hare University are still under-privileged. They have a rotten library. We saw the (white) librarian. One of our party said to him that they didn't seem to have any law books; perhaps we could organise a way of collecting some in the United Kingdom and sending them some to help them build up a better basic stock? No, said the librarian, if we had any law books here, the black students would just steal them anyway. The student president, who had taken us to see the library was himself a black student reading Law, and was standing listening to this conversation. If I had been him, I think I would have clouted that stupid, insensitive and rude librarian. What he actually said was something like, "I don't condone any stealing, of course, but if you got copies of the necessary books in the library for law students, I will guarantee they will not steal them." He told me later that most black students' families couldn't afford to pay their fees, not even their board. And a tutor said to me, "How do you advise a student who isn't doing her work properly, when she tells you she hasn't eaten anything for three days?"

The future is not simple. Our future is not easy to look forward to. Yet Advent is a time for confidence, confidence in God, confidence in ourselves. If they can show amazing hope in South Africa, at least I ought to be able to try a little better, here. After all, I am not going to starve, nor even have to do without the odd book or two that I want. The future is scary, right enough. We shall have to be prepared for deterioration, for sadness, for death – even for Christmas! Advent is about preparing, and preparing in confidence can be fun. Finding those things you haven't seen for 12 months, sifting out what is important from what isn't. Preparing ourselves.

There's a story about Winston Churchill. When he was 80, someone asked him if he were prepared to meet his maker. He's supposed to have replied, "I am ready to meet my maker; whether my maker is ready for the great ordeal of meeting me is quite another matter!" And Voltaire, when he was dying, is said to have been asked whether, having been a famous atheist all his life, was he now prepared to renounce the devil. He said he didn't think this was a good time to be making new enemies! Advent is a time for preparing, and preparing can be good – even preparing to die. Living, after all, is a terminal disease. It is worth preparing. It used to be common to sing grace before meals —"Praise God from whom all blessings flow." But it's the second verse of Bishop Thomas Ken's hymn I value:

Redeem thy mis-spent time that's past
Live this day as if it were thy last;
Improve thy talent with due care
For the great day thyself prepare.

It's no bad aim for Advent: to get into the habit of preparing. You don't have to sleep in a coffin every night to learn to prepare for the ending of life, as monks have sometimes done. But we can use other opportunities to prepare, even if we are never absolutely prepared for anything, never mind dying. For Advent is about confidence in our preparing. For some people, preparing for Christmas seems to begin very early indeed, these days. Preparing can be more fun than the real thing.

PSALM

1. In the darkness I wait with excitement:
    light will bring Christmas and happiness for us all.
2. But darkness is needed as a prelude to light:
    and night-time must come before day.
3. In the middle of darkest winter, light begins to return:
    after dying, the seed can spring to life.
4. So Christ comes in at Christmastime:
    the shortest day brings hope for the future.
5. In the darkness I wait in trembling:
    for the light will show up what is wrong.
6. I haven't used the opportunities you give:
    so much of my life has been missing the mark.
7. The Lord will come - he will not be slow:
    his herald offers justice for all people in the world.
8. Christ comes now in judgement:
    and he judges in truth but with mercy.
9. In the darkness I wait with longing:
    candlelight is flanking the bread and wine.
10. All that I have is represented at your altar:
    all that I am is offered to you.
11. In return you give me yourself:
    the bread of your body for the health of my soul.

12. Christ is present in the Eucharist:
    make yourself known in the breaking of bread.

13. In the darkness I wait with expectation:
    for tomorrow is always uncertain.

14. We look for your goodness to be renewed:
    when all things are finally ended.

15. Death will be swallowed up in victory:
    the grave will no longer be the end.

16. Christ will come as the end for all creation:
    even so, come to us, Lord Jesus.

17. In the darkness I wait in confidence:
    anticipating presents, the signs of love.

18. Decorations are symbols of hopefulness:
    the scurrying points to imminent judgement.

19. Whatever you have in store, I am your servant:
    may everything be done in accordance with your will.

20. Christ, come in at Christmastime:
    bring in your just yet gentle rule.

ADVENT – the end time.

It used to be the tradition to keep the four Sundays of Advent, by remembering the great themes of the end times – death, judgement, heaven and hell. There's scope for the hell-fire sermon, if ever there was one. I think I have only heard such preaching once, and in Scotland. It rests, of course, on the assumption that these pictures of the end are, in some sense at least, literally true. That is why they are so scary. And fundamentalism of that kind is, fortunately, out of fashion at present. There are those who say that September 11th 2001 has changed the world for ever. It is not easy to know what people mean by that. If it is simply that we are more conscious of our mortality, of the message of Advent, that is fine. If they mean that we need to get back to a more fundamentalist literal understanding of what awaits us after death, then I have to be very worried.

Naturally, though, I am biased. I was told, when training for ordination, that I was not fit to be a minister of the Gospel because I did not believe in "life-after-death." So I was sent away from my college to change my mind. I am even more certain now that, for many, if not most, good Christian people, the faith we believe has little to do with God but a great deal to do with what we think happens to us

23

after we have died. I do not believe that is what Jesus was really preaching, nor do I think it is what the Christian faith is primarily about; it comes in only the last sentences in the Creeds, most of which is about God the Holy Trinity. A great disservice was done to Christmas by the song made popular by Boney M that declares "Man shall live for ever more, because of Christmas Day." It's sometimes said that what most Christians, indeed I suspect most people, really believe in is the doctrine of the immortality of the soul. There is a part of us, the Inner Light or something, which never will go out; our bodies will fade away and deteriorate even if they do not collapse in an instant, but our souls will go marching on. By contrast, the Christian doctrine is of the resurrection of the body. That means that we will really die. But, by sheer grace, those who are chosen will rise again, when Christ comes back on the last day, and the chosen will be given a new body. That body is not, as St Paul points out, the same body we would all recognise from life on earth, but a completely different kind of body. It is, oddly enough, more akin to re-incarnation than to the immortality of the soul. But few Christians there are who seem to believe it!

The medieval ideas of judgement, heaven and hell are made clear in the Mystery Plays, especially as I remember them at York in the grounds of St Mary's Abbey. The top of the Abbey ruins was heaven, where God was, with a few angels (but not anybody else, interestingly enough!). The stage was earth where Adam was created and the devil was sent down to, and where Jesus was born and crucified. Under the stage was where everyone went when we die, and to which the risen Christ went, on the last day, to rescue the souls of the righteous for a life in heaven and consigned the rest to hell for eternal punishment. It's a wonderful picture. But I wonder if it was it ever meant to be taken literally. We know the "three-decker universe" is a powerful picture, telling much that is true, but it is hardly an accurate portrayal of what is going to happen to us all after death.

The message of death, judgement, heaven and hell must be about how we live, not about something that we might expect the day after we die. Sartre used the phrase "hell is other people" and we may well think that heaven is, too. The pictures are not to tell us what to expect in our personal future, but how to behave now. And it is clear to me, from how most Christian people behave, that we do not believe in life-after-death anyway. We cling firmly, indeed obstinately, on to life, and make it crystal clear that life is everything and death to be avoided. We do not live as if we believed in a future life of bliss or punishment ahead of us. Apparently terrorists from a Muslim background do sometimes believe in paradise for martyrs in the cause, so they are perfectly happy to kill themselves as well as infidels. I have never met a Christian using that argument and indeed I should be happy if more Muslims publicly denounced it, too, as it is an aberration. In one sense, it may be thought to be similar to what Jesus was doing by engineering his own crucifixion, but in his case he was perpetrating no violence but simply allowing others to commit violence on him. There are those Christians who say that death is "the last great adventure" because they do not know what happens afterwards, and are keen to discover. But that is not the same as taking the pictures of heaven and hell literally. The best we can make of it is to say we do not know.

If the final judgement, heaven and hell are picture language, what might the reality be? At the least, they provide us with language to explain that everything we do in this life is important, that we face judgement daily, and that we are aware of heaven and hell in our own experiences. A friend of mine once put it in a "thought for the day" in the local paper, and I cannot now remember his words, but they were similar to these:

I believe
that love is stronger than hate
that peace is more lasting than war
that life is more powerful than death
that caring for others is more fulfilling than selfishness
that talking is more productive than violence
that faith begins with self-confidence
and that the stories of Jesus provide a focus for my
understanding and reflection

Stories of Harry Potter and the Lord of the Rings are very influential, but no-one tries to think they are some kind of image of precisely what did happen in some past time or distant place, although they speak powerfully of what we experience in our own lives. For reasons I do not understand, we seem to expect to do just the opposite with the images and stories of religion. My daughter had the right idea, I thought, when she dismissed my attempt to explain Robin Hood (I think it was) and said "Oh but that's only history not the real story."

PSALM

1. "I am the beginning and the ending":
   the Mystery Plays begin and end with God.

2. In the beginning you made whatever there is:
   you created the universe and everything that's in it.

3. Humanity is the crown of all creation:
   in your image you made them, male and female,

4. for Adam and Eve it was paradise:
   but disobedience spoilt it,
   and the feeling of shame led to punishment.

5. Abraham's obedience was tested in sacrifice:
   he believed in you enough to give up his only son.

6. By obedience, Mary became your servant:
   Jesus was born, the child of promise.

7. Shepherds brought the homage of ordinary people:
   and kings from the east worshipped
   with their treasures.

8. John the baptizer was the last of the prophets:
   Jesus presented himself for baptism.

9. His teaching brought many to the kingdom of heaven:
   your healing came through him to all sorts of people;

10. crowds of supporters welcomed him into Jerusalem:
    but he drove the dealers out of the Temple.

11. Church leaders wanted to put him away:
    the political masters showed little respect;

12. Jesus was killed for the sin of the world:
    all who passed saw him die and understood the reasons.

13. His disciples found him alive and risen:
    those who'd been closest to him knew he had conquered.

14. Even the dead were aroused by his voice:
    the devils heard it and were terrified.

15. At doomsday, the wicked are consigned to torment:
    but all the obedient are raised to glory.

16. So the plays present the story of the world:
    it's our obedience to God from beginning to end.

EVERY STEP OF THE WAY

THREE

MEETING JESUS AGAIN

CHRISTMAS

Christmas, despite our frantic parties and shopping, actually does not begin until midnight on Christmas Eve, and goes on for the 12 days of Christmas (which are after Christmas) and for the 40 days of the season which end on February 2nd, the festival of Candlemas.

Once upon a time, there was a man called Ben Smith (actually, his proper name was Ebenezer, but he tried not to use that in public). Everyone knew that Ben was a self-centred man and that he lived very well, thank you. He had three cars, several televisions and all the latest state-of-the-art hi-fi. He had at least two freezers and two lawn mowers (and, of course, a little man who would work them). He used to live in Church Street, but he got fed up with the sound of the church bells, so he moved out to live in a more rural atmosphere where he wouldn't be worried by noise, and where religion wouldn't bother him so much. He invested his money and never gave away a penny of it, unless there was a hope of some return.

One of his employees was a man called Bob Crighton. He had a happy family but not much money; in fact his pay was less than just and never rose above the legal limit that his firm could get away with. The Crightons were used to spending any money they did have on other people – the grandparents, taking friends out, and they always reckoned that, for every pound they got, 10 pence was put aside for Christian Aid, Oxfam, Shelter, or the church envelopes.

At Christmas, Ben Smith spent hundreds of pounds. Any business people he wanted to cultivate were given generous presents. In fact, many people thought he was a naturally generous man. Of course, he never gave anything much to his own family – he had lost touch with most of them, anyway. He never had anything to do with religion – that was all humbug, he said, only for hypocrites. He felt that churches and mosques and temples were only there to spoil people's fun. He was an unhappy man.

fun. He was an unhappy man.

The Crightons never spent very much on Christmas. In fact, they frequently had to make sure they did not spend as much as they had done the year before. They usually shared their turkey with people who might not otherwise have had a Christmas dinner, or who would otherwise have spent Christmas on their own. Their presents tended to be useful. They felt that Christmas was about Jesus and about being happy – and happiness isn't something you can pay for and get delivered.

You know the story well enough, of course. I have been ticked off for using it at Christmas time, because I was simply making everyone feel guilty instead of good. Perhaps the (night) cap fits too well. Charles Dickens was an expert at making the cap fit. But I tell the story so that it fits me, as well. There is a great deal for us to feel guilty about. Christmas so often seems hidden by the darkness of wars, fear, violence, hunger and homelessness. Some people say that Christmas is hidden by money – it is commercialisation, they say. Yet we cannot go back to a time when it was not so. In 1843, after all, things were just as bad, or the story wouldn't have become so popular.

But there is some light. Murphy thought the light at the end of the tunnel was only the headlamp of the oncoming train. But there is some real light, too. And it gives light to anyone who is prepared to look. Money is a problem, and especially if it comes in packages of several million pounds at a time. The family at Bethlehem is seen as the ultimate happy family, but they had no mod. cons., never mind money. The light is that God speaks to you – usually silently, very silently. The real light is that God is with us, always. That in the mess and chaos and unfairness we live in, God is beside us. All we have to do is to make room – a space for God's word, room for God's presence, and a thank you. The real light is here for everyone, and comes even to your world at Christmas.

PSALM

1. God loved people, so you came to live among us:
   you care for us all, and you will be with us always;

2. your light shines on, in the darkness that surrounds us:
   as the sun turns back on its course towards the summer.

3. The longest night is over and the future is brighter:
   bitter cold may still come, but the springtime will follow,

4. so the darkness in our hearts you have conquered for ever:

5. As the evergreen tree lives on through the winter:
    so your love wins through to us, whatever may befall;
6. throughout the bleakest day,
    we can warm ourselves with confidence:
    for God's Son has shown us
    he has power over everything.
7. God still loves people, and sustains us every day:
    you care for us all, and you will help us always.
8. For you speak to us gently,
    in our shopping and preparing:
    your judgement presses down on us,
    yet with understanding.
9. Hectic activity may blot out our deepest worries:
    but you are closest to us in our quiet and aloneness,
10. because your life on earth was forever
    marked by loneliness:
    you know our depressions and our sense of isolation.
11. But even in festivities we needn't just ignore you:
    you take part in our weddings and in all our
    celebrations.
12. In company, and by myself, you are always present:
    for God's Son has sympathy with all our human
    feelings.
13. God will love people and be closer to us always:
    you care for us all, and you'll lead us on for ever.
14. Family festivals can point to you like road signs:
    the commercial world can show us how to love
    ourselves and others.
15. Each year at Christmas, there is more for us to learn:
    the enjoyment of children can help us
    become more child-like,
16. for we can see your face in the wonderment of children:
    in the need of the poor and the joy of the secure.
17. Wise men recognise your ever guiding hand:
    for you are always with us,
    leading on to new discoveries.
18. Glory to God and in the world there will be peace:
    for your Son shows you love us
    and your love embraces everyone.

CHRISTMAS - the meaning

We've been waiting ... waiting for Christmas to come, waiting for God, perhaps. And then at Christmas, the waiting is over, and it's here.

You know how it is when you turn up to the party wearing your ordinary clothes, and you find that everyone else is wearing fancy dress. Worse still, when you find everyone's wearing T-shirt and jeans and you're the only one wearing the Father Christmas outfit (or more often, the tie, or the clerical collar, or the suit). Well, when that happens, there's usually nothing you can do about it. It's tough. Well, it's the same when Christmas arrives, and there's nothing we can do to change anything. It's too late. At least we have arrived.

We arrive at Christmas as we are. The shepherds were in their working clothes, the kings in their dressy garb. The baby won't mind whatever you are wearing. Babies don't notice. This one doesn't ever notice something as silly as the clothes we wear. We arrive to remember what we are worth to the baby at Bethlehem ... you are not worth simply what your clothes declare about you. (You are worth far more than even the most expensive clothes could show.) You are not worth just what your Christmas present is worth (it may be gold, or it may be a lamb, but you are worth far more than any present). You are not worth what you have in the bank − not even if it's the £11 million you've just won on the Lottery. You are worth more than any amount of money.

We put the two stories of Christmas together, as if they fitted. The church has often tried to keep the kings for January, but it doesn't really work. Everybody wants to see them as part of the Christmas story, and we don't want to wait for a week or more (when, for many of us, Christmas is "over"). For the Gospel stories are not merely stories for children, but theology for adults. The Matthew Gospel is the one written for Jewish people. It's about proving from the Jewish scriptures that Jesus is the Christ, the Messiah expected by the prophecies from the past. Joseph is descended from King David. The angel of God comes to tell Joseph about his son who is to be born, and he has to be born in Bethlehem (and be male) in order to fulfil the prophecies about the Jews' Messiah. The rich and powerful wise men see a heavenly message in the stars and they are led to Bethlehem, the city of David, where they find the Holy Family and present their treasures. The Luke Gospel is written for Gentile Christians, so it presents the same message but in a very different way. It is to show how God cares for non-Jews, for outsiders, including women. So the angel comes to Mary to tell her about her son who is to be born. The heavenly message in the skies comes to shepherds, working men, who are regarded as outsiders for they are not even able to keep the Sabbath because of their work. It is they who are led to Bethlehem to find the Holy Family and to offer their own kind of treasure, which is so very different, poor words merely which Mary treasures in her heart. The stories are not historical facts about what happened, they are there to tell the same story about God. Although the Luke Gospel tries to tell the story as if it were history (in our sense), it manages to get the dates wrong! The gospel says that Jesus was born when Herod was King and Quirinius was Governor of Syria. Unfortunately, however, Quirinius began in 6 CE while Herod had already died ten years before in 4 BCE. Nor can you easily arrive at a date from the other stories of the journey of astrologers, following a star, or co-incidence of planets. It took until the 4th century of the Christian era before December 25th began to be recognised as the festival of the birth of Jesus. It was the Roman festival of the birthday of the unconquered sun, taken over to celebrate the Son. The best agreement may be that Jesus was born in the autumn of 4 BCE. Nevertheless, we tell the stories to children, because of their magic brilliance. To use the words of Dominic Crossan, "none of this ever happened, of course, but it's true nonetheless."

At Christmas, God is saying YES to you. Never mind whether you have the right clothes, or the right money, or the right present. There's an old Christian tradition: that God sends each one of us into the world with a special message to deliver, a special song to sing for others, a special act of love to give. No one else can speak your message, or sing your song, or offer your act of love. That is entrusted only to you. So no matter what gift you may bring (you may be a bit ashamed of it), no matter what clothes you wear (you may see you've got the fashion wrong), no matter what money you don't have, the baby can't see. Your special gift is the only one that matters to him. (It's a pity the same can't always be said of our Christmas gifts to one another, too!)

PSALM

1. We are travellers on the road to seek you today:
    the stories of Christmas are stories of journeys.

2. Mary and Joseph had to travel to Bethlehem:
    the holy family were pilgrims before Christ could come.

3. The shepherds decided to go and see:
    working people went to find where God was at work.

4. Wise men followed the pointing star:
    kings from far away seeking truth from above.

31

5.   Christ still comes to us where we are:
>but we also must seek him in response to his love,

6.   our journey may begin at any time or place:
>you will lead the way for us and you will sustain us.

7.   So help us travel our own road of faith:
>that we may see for ourselves, and believe in you.

CHRISTMAS – worse every year?

It was in the High Street a week or two before Christmas, when I met a lady I knew because she worked in one of the local shops. She seemed very 'down' and I asked her why she was so depressed when it was nearly Christmas. Shouldn't she be feeling more excited and happy, at this time of year? She explained that it was because of the presents she had to get for her two small children. Last year, she had spent £500 on them, so this year she was going to have to spend more than that, and she couldn't really afford it. They would be very disappointed if she didn't spend more than last year on them.

George MacLeod used to tell the story about a Glasgow church where the stained glass window had been broken by a stone. The inscription should have read "Glory to God in the Highest," but it actually read "High St." He felt that, on the whole, the text had been improved by the stone throwing! It is in the ordinary, the depressions as well as the joys, the shopping and the chores, in those normal events that we are to look for God, not just in churches and angels and the extraordinary world we experience on few occasions in our lives.

In a way, the same kind of thing had happened to the Jewish people in the Bible. First, they had experienced the immense power of God working for them in the great miracle of the Exodus from Egypt. That extraordinary event was told again every year of their lives. Later, through the reigns of David and Solomon, their life had become very secure and comfortable. The Temple of God was built and Solomon was renowned throughout the world of his time for his great wealth and glory. But things went wrong. People became disobedient, and the prophets said it was their fault for disobeying God. They were driven into exile and the Temple was destroyed. The pressure seemed to be on, and every year just got a little bit worse. In the end, their country was under occupation by the Romans, their kings were mere puppets, and there wasn't too much justice in evidence, nor mercy. They needed another Exodus, really. And then Jesus was born, whose name meant he was to be the "saviour" of his people. From a Christian perspective, Christmas happened when things were pretty bad. All through Jesus's life, looking back at it, he must have felt the same. God seemed to act only when things were bleak.

Yet we often feel as if the opposite ought to be true. We expect silence and peace in order to worship, we expect to find praying easy when things are going well for us, we assume that we shall never die or fail (and if we do, it isn't fair!). So maybe the Christmas rush could be good for us. It might remind us that God acts when the pressure is on, not just in the peace and silence. God is with us when we don't have time to think, when we are feeling down and alone. It may be difficult for us to "say our prayers" at such times. Yet the real prayer may be just the experience of things going badly. For God's moment is often closer to us than we think. Christmas happens, not by accident, at the darkest time of the year, and Christ was born at midnight.

PSALM

1. Is there no justice in the world:
   why do some of us have such a hard journey?

2. Christmas is the time for family joy:
   it's also the time of the greatest misery.

3. When troubles come, they don't arrive alone:
   we often hear of three disasters;

4. there are those who have more than their fair deserts:
   it's not just that some are accident prone.

5. Your promise is to let us face no more than we can handle:
   your Spirit gives us strength to cope with
   everything that comes;

6. you give us your presence and your understanding:
   in Jesus you have known and experience our afflictions.

7. We need to come to terms with our traumas:
   every anniversary is painful, but surviving it helps us
   live on.

8. New friends are made through accidents:
   those who know how we feel can best support us.

9. There's no answer to the question 'why?':
   but, if you are with me, I can find a way forward.

EPIPHANY

What is the answer to all the questions of life, the universe and everything? If you are an addict of the Hitchhiker's Guide to the Galaxy, you will know that the answer is 42. There is a story of the man who was looking for the answer to life and searched everywhere for it. Eventually someone told him that the person to see was a particular guru in India. So he travelled as cheaply as he could and struggled to find the person who would give him the answer. When he did find the right guru, he asked his important question, and he was told, "Agree with everything that anyone says." The man was quite angry. He shouted that he hadn't travelled all this way to be told he had to agree with everyone. That's not the answer to all the questions of life, he said. And the guru replied, "You are right. That is not the answer to all the questions of life."

Well, I'll tell you what the answer is. It is that everything is a gift. Just like Christmas presents. Everything we have, everything we receive, even our life itself is given to us. Like gold, frankincense and myrrh. Some things are gifts you like very much indeed (like gold). Others are not much use, but they make you feel better (like incense). Some presents are positively horrible (like myrrh with all its bad associations) – sometimes, thankfully, you can take them back to Marks and Spencer's; sometimes you can't. Some things that we have, too, are gifts we just have to live with. But everything we have and are is a gift.

Why is this the answer to anything? Well, because nowadays it often seems that the first response we make to anything is that it must be somebody (else)'s fault. Driving my car the other day, I was following a car that slowed down where it was in the middle of the road. When I was about to overtake it, one flick of the indicator and the car suddenly turned right. I was frightened; it could have been quite nasty. So I became angry, in a way that I'm sure I never used to be! Perhaps we have learned to be selfish, part of a consumer society in which I can have anything I want. As Ivan Boesky put it in the 1980s, "It's OK to be greedy." And if anyone gets in my way, then they are wrong. So we have learned to blame somebody for everything. Not me, of course; I am always right; it's the other person who is to blame!

That is why it seems that the answer to our questions is to see everything as a gift. Or, to put it in the words of the New Testament, "it is by grace we are saved." We don't deserve what we have become, or what happens to us, it is by grace – a present, not always a present we are going to enjoy, but grace nonetheless. We tend to notice gifts only when they are good, like the day I was searching for money to pay for the car park, and a lady driving out put her hand out of the car window. "We're not staying," she said, "have our ticket." It was a gift. When we can learn to accept the good gifts (the gold), then we can begin to learn to receive the myrrh as well.

PSALM

1. It's always exciting to receive a gift:
    this day is your gift to me, for all comes from you.

2. The wise men offered their gifts at Bethlehem:
    we present ourselves to you
    and our lives for your hallowing -

3. the gold of our precious time:
    the worship and incense of our talents,

4. the costly ointment of our money:
    for the love of money is deadly myrrh.

5. The journey of the magi was long and heavy going:
    we too look for a leader, for the meaning of living,

6. the reason we give for our search is that
    we may be loving:
    and our journey also is long, till we become human.

7. Now we've settled back to routine
    after Christmas is over:
    the usual daily round and life as before.

8. Children may search for the hidden kings:
    but we are all of us seekers
    in the quest for your kingdom.

9. We offer to you new gifts on our pilgrimage:
    excited by the gifts we've received,
    through your loving grace.

EPIPHANY – the good news

Once upon a time, I used to remember the words of the Bible. There was only one version in English (what we now call the King James Version) and we were encouraged to learn bits of it by heart. It was perhaps rather like the way Muslims are expected to learn the Koran, not necessarily to understand any of its message, just learn it by heart. Nowadays, we find it much harder to learn the Bible. There are too many differences. Yet the differences can teach us how to begin to understand it.

Every Step of the Way

"Glory to God in the highest," sang the angels, "and on earth peace goodwill among men." I sometimes used to worry that it wasn't very good news. What about the women, for a start? For another thing, peace and goodwill don't just arrive, they have to be worked for, and that work can be very frustrating. It means people will probably need restraining, and may well be hurt. Goodwill to all is not good news. "Glory to God in the highest heaven," it says in one modern version, "and on earth peace to those with whom he is pleased." That's fine, except for those with whom God is not pleased, and there must be some of them around, if not just me. Because we all feel we have upset God sometimes! A better version might be, "Glory to God on high, and to humanity with whom God is pleased." It's because God loves us all that Christmas happened. That sounds more like good news for everyone.

And yet... The world is not a place to please God, or anyone. There is still far too much that is not peace at all, from the Middle East and every continent to the family and our own heart. In the 1960s people thought that peace was just around the corner. President John Kennedy said, "Most people look at the world and ask 'why?' I dream about what the world might be and ask 'why not?'" We all know the story of the devout lady who prayed every day that Jesus might come, and one Christmas she seemed to hear him saying that he would come that day. "I shall be ready for you," she said. She cleaned the house and polished the furniture, making sure that everything was in its right place. There was a knock at the door, and she rushed to open it. But there stood the local tramp, whom she knew very well, asking for a mince pie. She said she was very sorry, but couldn't invite him in, because she was expecting a very special visitor, so she quickly gave him a mince pie and sent him away. She waited for the time to come, but no one came. In her prayer, that night, she complained that Jesus had not come as he promised, and she seemed to hear his voice say to her, "Oh yes, I did come, but you said that someone important was expected and sent me away."

So perhaps the good news is that God is present in his world, but we do not notice. God is there in all the mess and muddle that we know only too well, but we are too busy looking somewhere else! The message of epiphany is that we shall find God if we look. For he is here. Emmanuel, "God is with us."

PSALM

1. God you are around me always:
   your presence continually surrounds me.

2. I don't see you, but I know you are there:
   I can't feel you, yet I'm aware of your attendance.

3. The servant of your prophet could not see:
   the young man's eyes were blinded to your closeness.

4. Elisha prayed for his eyes to be opened:
   and you showed him your power surrounding them.

5. So show us your encircling presence:
   the epiphany of your protection and care;

6. then we shall worship you and bring you our gifts:
   our goods, our prayers, and our lives in your service.

7. At times when I am frightened,
   make me feel you're in command:
   and when I have to be alone,
   help me know your abiding company.

CANDLEMAS

The fact that this is exactly 40 days after midnight on Christmas Eve is no accident. It marks the end of the Christmas season (or, if you prefer, the end of the Epiphany season – Christmas lasting for the "twelve days" from Christmas Day to 12th night on January 6th, the festival of the Epiphany). Candlemas is marked with a story of Jesus as a baby being "presented" in the Temple at Jerusalem. Another unlikely event, if ever there was one, but told by the Luke Gospel with an abundance of meaning. The Luke Gospel likes to provide one story for men followed by another for women. This tells us the story of a man, followed by that of a woman, and how they recognised the Messiah in a helpless small baby.

In order to be "purified," Mary had to go to church. Not just her local synagogue, but the Holy City, for the Gospel is saying that they were a religious family, who kept the Law. It is not very fashionable nowadays to keep the traditional rules, nor even to go to church! Nor was this a festival for the Blessed Virgin, merely, but more like a religious duty for the whole family. It was Mary who came away pondering; we are not told what Joseph thought (but this is the Luke Gospel's emphasis again). Or maybe Joseph didn't have "religious experiences." How often we, too, go to church reluctantly, perhaps, and come away having been made to think, and to worship; how often we go willingly, expecting to come away pondering, and find we have not had the experience we expected!

The old man Simeon saw the baby and made up the Nunc Dimittis, so that we could sing it at Evensong for the next 2,000 years. Well, never mind the history, what is the point? Simeon said, in his prayer, that God could now let him die because he had seen all he ever wanted. There's a sign of faith for you. There is nothing about how he wanted to meet all his relatives who had died before him; nothing about how he was looking forward to heaven; just gratitude for what he had been allowed to see – the most important person of all time, both for Jews and for non Jews. When you can hand over that much to God, there's faith for you. No prayers, no requests, just let go. That is, perhaps, why the words often seem so appropriate at a funeral. Then there is the story of the old lady Anna who had not retired, even at the age of 84. We are told she just happened to be passing, and she began to praise God. Not complaining about her arthritis, not telling Simeon off for not helping with the washing up, just praising. Of course, it's also true that people who are not yet 84 can sometimes fall into the trap of praising God instead of doing the equivalent of the washing up. But, nevertheless, there is a lesson for us, to learn to praise God when we see a baby, or anyone, or any thing. All is thanksgiving.

PSALM

1. Here I am, mother, at your bidding:
   your obedience is a pattern for me to follow,

2. for a mother knows what it is to be hurt:
   to live for another, so they may develop.

3. All blessings to you among women and men:
   full of grace and strength, help us also to grow;

4. glorious among all who have gone before us:
   you are given honour as Queen of Heaven.

5. We are all children of Eve our mother:
   we ask you, holy mother, show us Jesus your son.

6. Mother of God, I look to you for support:
   to see God through your eyes, Mary most holy.

7. You stood by the cross with your son at his dying:
   be with me now for I need God's power.

8. You felt the sword that was piercing your heart:
   pray for me today as I face my trials.

EVERY STEP OF THE WAY

FOUR

THE CRUCIAL TIME

ASH WEDNESDAY

In preparation for the great festival of Easter, we have six weeks of Lent starting on Ash Wednesday, a reminder of our mortality. For this "Forty Days" leads up to the holiest time of all, the remembrance of the suffering and death of Jesus on a criminal's cross.

There is a powerful but very old story – about Parsifal and the Fisher King. The old king held the secret of the Holy Grail. But he had become ill. Everything was dying with him – the springs had no water, the plants had stopped growing, animals had stopped breeding and even the palace walls were beginning to crumble into dust. Knights came from far and wide to visit and ask kindly about the old king. But then one knight came, different from the others; he was decrepit and ridiculous, and had not even bothered to clean himself up after his journey … Parsifal. He did not stop to enquire about the king, but went straight in without observing any of the courtly etiquette. He went directly to the old king and said, "Where is the Holy Grail?" At the question, the old king got up, cured. The streams began to flow, the animals to breed, the plants to grow, and even the palace walls were restored.

I suppose the point of the story is that asking the right question gives all of us a second chance. We believe in a God who gives second chances. "Return to the Lord who will have mercy: to our God who will richly pardon." (Isaiah 55.7)

So the beginning of Lent is a time to take stock. Forty days (not counting the Sundays) is a reminder of the preparation of Jesus for his ministry, the forty days in the wilderness. It refers back to the preparation of Israel in their forty years of wandering in the desert. For the Christian, this is a time to enter into the experiencing of the death of Christ so that we may be raised with him at the great festival of Easter. To begin the preparation is a recall, to "return to the Lord."

PSALM OF CONFESSION

1. I know there are times when I'm sinful:
    for sin lies waiting by my footsteps every day.

2. But 'sin' is not a word we use very often:
    what's against the law may not be sinful, after all;

3. the law may be clear in its rulings:
    but the greatest error lies in being found out!

4. Yet a mistake doesn't make me feel guilty:
    I get away with many things, still I'm not a sinner.

5. Nevertheless I'm often conscious of shame:
    I know that I do not like myself,

6. because I have missed the mark:
    or in aiming too low I have found the target.

7. "Remember you are dust and to dust you shall return:
    turn away from sin and be faithful to Christ."

8. There's always more that needs to be done:
    sins of omission are more than those I have committed.

9. Repentance means seeing myself in your eyes:
    in your presence I feel like running away from you.

10. "Only accept that you are unacceptable:
    and accept the fact that you are accepted."

11. Just as I am, I come to you for cleansing:
    wash me in your Spirit and help me to grow

LENT

There was a time when good Christian people kept the 40 days of Lent. We went to church more often, some people went daily. We tried to remember the season by giving up something we enjoyed, like chocolate (and we probably spent most of the time arguing with ourselves about whether we had given up chocolate, or maybe just chocolates – so this chocolate biscuit would be "all right" after all). It has become much more difficult to make Lent into a season of "abstinence" or fasting. It is even longer than Ramadan and kept far less enthusiastically! So, these days, we sometimes remit the 40 days to a shorter time"– Passiontide, perhaps, just a fortnight; or just a week,–"Holy Week" as we call it, with its own special rhythm and story. Keeping Holy Week was probably the first attempt at keeping a Christian calendar. Originally, it had simply been Sunday, the weekly memorial of Easter, the single annual festival. But after the time of Constantine (in the fourth century) there was already beginning to be an extension to Easter, the keeping of a holy week of preparation.

Indeed, Lent originated in a spring festival, when the daylight is lentening, or lengthening, a time of rejoicing in new growth or seed sowing. Even before the keeping of Holy Week, there was a time for the preparation of those who were to be baptised at Easter. Later on there was a similar period for penitents, observing Lent as a preparation for their re-admission to communion at Easter. There is, of course, a connection between Lent as a time of deepening discipleship and the spring. Perhaps it should be a season for taking up things, rather than for giving up things, anyway? Or perhaps a time for deepening the experience we already have of God. Giving up something small, like sugar in coffee or going to the shops in the car, or watching the telly while you're eating your tea, is a token. So that, especially when we forget to do it, we are reminded of God who has done so much for us. Taking something up might be a series of meetings laid on for us, or reading a book, or taking time to pray. And for the same reason, to remind us how much God has already done for us.

The Archbishop of Paris, I think it was who told a story of a group of young boys who had been determined to take the silly old parish priest for a ride. They tried to work out a way of making him look as silly as they knew he really was. So it was decided that one of them would go into church, at confession time, and make a bogus confession. Just to fool the old boy. But the old boy was not so foolish as they thought. He listened to the bogus confession, and explained that, after it was over, the boy was expected to make a simple act of penance. He said, "What I ask you to do is just to go and stand beneath the big cross on the screen, with the figure of Jesus crucified on it. Just look up at that figure for a while and then say, slowly, to yourself, 'You did all this for me, and I couldn't care a toss,' just that." The boy thought this would be a lark, so he went up to the crucifix and looked at it, "You did all this for me," he said. And then, he stopped. It didn't feel quite so silly, after all. And the Archbishop used to end the story by saying, "I know that story is true, because that little boy was me."

PSALM

1.   Do not be frightened or worried:
        for I am your God and I'm always beside you.
2.   Be determined and confident:
        since you are mine I will always support you.

3.   I am the God of love who moves on gently:
        leading you on,
        drawing you into all that is new and lovely.

4.   All you need is available now:
        let me carry you and bear you along in safety.

5.   I am the Lord of love who comes to you in quietness:
        there's no need for struggle or panic,

6.   for I died for you in the cruelty of torture:
        how can I let you suffer alone?

7.   I am the Spirit of love to direct you tenderly:
        I hold your hand and I will not hurry you.

8.   We will go on together into tomorrow:
        for I am with you and I won't let you go.

9.   Be not afraid for I am with you:
        I shall never abandon you wherever you may fall.

10. Only be strong and very courageous:
        for you are mine and I will always love you.

PASSIONTIDE

Once upon a time, we belonged to Britain. We knew we all belonged together. The enemy was Hitler, perhaps, or just life. If we were short of something, we borrowed or begged it from our neighbours. If someone died, we all joined in to buy a wreath, and we all went to see and to support the bereaved family. And the Royal Family was a kind of symbol of our unity, at the head of the country. The Church was (at least the Church of England, of Scotland, in Wales, or of Ireland) not exactly united in the United Kingdom, but certainly a church for the nation.

It is not like that, any more. The Church of England, they say, like the Church in Wales, should be disestablished; then it would be able to make decisions about worship, as it wished, without having to wait for Parliament to ratify everything churches want to do, least of all a Prayer Book. We live in a pluralist society with people of many different religions, and of none. Politicians, perhaps, have not changed that much, but nowadays we can hear and see them, almost daily, shouting at one another, undermining one another, goading and blaming one another. If that's how our rulers behave, who's to say that the rest of us shouldn't behave the same way? You might say something similar about the Royals. We are no longer a people who belong to one another, but a people in conflict. Rich

42

against poor. Maybe it has always been like that, but we are only just becoming aware of it. Jesus wept over the city of Jerusalem. He weeps over us, too.

Perhaps it is my fault. I have often felt out of step with other people. I am used to feeling that other people are praying hard for my conversion to their way of thinking. I have nearly always lived in what was a 'safe' political seat, so it did not feel as if my vote would ever make any difference at all. I have often been aware of thinking that the dear old Church of England was continually making the wrong decisions, and all I could do was to lump it. I have often been aware of conflict. I don't like it very much. That is partly because it makes me feel, naturally enough, that I am right and the others are unfortunately just wrong. How arrogant! Now I am having to come to terms with a divided society, in which many, perhaps most, other people will do me out of a living, if they can. Indeed, I sometimes feel so insecure that I think the others might deprive me of my life, if I upset them. So I tend to become turned in on myself, eager to keep what I can for myself or my family, even selfish and greedy.

Jesus wept.
"If only you had known," he said. And he went into church and shouted at them. "You're not praying," he said, "you're robbing one another." And the church people plotted to see how they could stifle this voice, this weeping voice, this angry voice. The voice that said they were not able to recognise God's moment when it came. And Jesus taught. He taught ordinary people, those who didn't come to church perhaps, people nobody noticed, those nobody said thank you to. Those people listened to Jesus.

Do you know, I think they still do! I think we still do. When we are looking for God's moment in our daily lives. When we are struggling to find a meaning in the things that happen to us, and there doesn't seem to be much that makes any sense at all. When we talk to someone in the street, listen to a neighbour, lend a hand or a little sugar when they've run out next door. And if our Eucharist helps us look for God in ordinary down-to-earth things like bread and wine; if our prayers help us look for God in ordinary down-to-earth people, like those we meet tomorrow; if our church helps us look for God in ordinary down-to-earth places, like schools or shops, courts or coaches; if we begin to look for God's moment in our own lives … then, maybe, just maybe, Jesus can stop weeping.

PSALM FOR PALM SUNDAY

1. The sun shines out on our joyful procession:
    the spring comes with daffodils and branches of palm.

2. We rejoice to welcome the coming of our king:
    Jesus rides into our city with shouts of triumph.

3. For this is the week of all weeks:
    Holy Week is the pivot of all our faith.

4. Who is this king of glory riding to his death:
    who is this man of sorrows ignored in our urban world?

5. Our generation doesn't see him as he was in Palestine:
    but Christ is still present in our streets and in our homes.

6. This cross of palm we take out in our hands:
    so help us take up our cross in our daily lives.

THE CALVARY CROSS

There's a story of a king and a wise man. King Croesus was very rich and he showed Solon, the wise man from Athens, all his treasures. It was fantastic, and he was very comfortable and well looked after. He was proud of himself. "Now," he said to the wisest man in all the world, "who's the most fortunate person you know?" Solon thought for a moment, and then said it was Timon of Athens. Why? Because he had a happy family, watched his children grow up, and died gloriously on the battlefield, where there is still a monument with his name on it. Croesus wasn't going to be put off. "Well, who's the second most fortunate person in all the world?" Solon spoke about Cleobis and Biton from Argos who had won the Olympic gold medal, and had a happy life before they, too, had died. Croesus started getting a bit fed up, with the mention of all these little people he had never even heard the names of before now. What was so wonderful about them? Solon saw his problem, and gave his wise saying: "Call nobody happy until he has died," he said.

The point of the story is that Croesus very soon crashed. His son was killed in battle and he lost his great empire, and all his riches. He was not the happiest man alive, any more. There's a distinctly modern ring to this old story.

Today, the best thing to be is "happy "– that is, successful, with lots of good things and an expensive big house, and (most of all) to be alive. But what if you then crash, if you lose everything, if you lose your job, if you are found out in your bit of adultery on the side, if you are ill, and most of all if you die (for that you most certainly will)? Christian faith can deal with all of that:

> There are many who hang on the cross: not only the unsuccessful revolutionaries, prisoners, those condemned to death; not only the incurably sick, the complete failures, those who are weary of life and those who despair of themselves and of the world. There are many who hang on the cross: tormented by cares and oppressed by their fellow men, overwhelmed by demands and worn out by boredom, crushed by fear and poisoned by hatred, forgotten by friends and ignored by the media. Is not everyone in fact hanging on his own cross?
> (Hans Kung: On being a Christian: Collins. London 1977. p. 576)

Look at the cross of Christ. Even obviously senseless suffering and death can have a meaning. So anything you suffer can have meaning, too. When you do suffer, it is possible also to conquer it, so Christianity says:

(1)   you can bear it – not by seeking suffering, but enduring the normal, everyday suffering, your cross; you are to bear it, "take it up" and follow Christ;

(2)   you can fight it – not just bearing it, but joining the world wide fight against suffering, poverty, deprivation, disease and death;

(3)   you can use it – there is a vital Christian tradition of being able to make use of suffering, enabling you to grow towards greater maturity, and the stature of Christ.

Mind you, we have to be careful how we handle this tradition. Joanna Trollope makes the Rector's wife justly impatient with a husband who uses the tradition to excuse his inability to get the promotion he has been expecting, because suffering is part of his spiritual progress. How very English!

In St Helen's Church Abingdon is a 14th century painting; Christ crucified is nailed to a lily. It is a not uncommon medieval image. Bishop Richard Harries of Oxford apparently thought of it as shocking – beauty and the beast, a beautiful flower and bloody torture. Somehow to me it seems very like Julian of Norwich. She saw Christ crucified and the blood trickling down his face, and she said (in her rather weak Latin) "Benedicite, Domine!" Then she immediately saw Our Lady at her annunciation - the lily after the crucifix. Perhaps we are shocked because of the oxymoron, the contrasting images. Perhaps we should be just as shocked by the idea of suffering and glory, of the victory of the Cross, being able to see the vicious suffering and torture and say, "Praise the Lord!"

45

PSALM

1.   Anger and frustration are in the air we breathe:
       our world has always been full of violence.

2.   Guns and knives are in evidence on our streets:
       human life is cheap in an expensive market place.

3.   These days I'm afraid of the city:
       subways are dark and threatening places.

4.   There are footsteps behind, people are following me:
       two men seem kind enough ... until we are alone.

5.   Why, God, why does this happen to me:
       what have I done to merit your fury?

6.   These are criminals and go free:
       there's no justice in the world you've made!

7.   I thought it was only others who were
       victims of violence:
       why do you bring this on me for no good reason?

8.   Why, God, why does this happen to me:
       it isn't fair when I've done nothing to deserve it.

9.   Animals kill to satisfy their hunger:
       but people are murderers for no reason at all,

10. they maim and beat others for fun:
       they've not been hurt or threatened by me.

11. Perhaps I am simply a symbol:
       I stand for the comfortable life they cannot share;

12. or else it was all a mistake:
       maybe I just happened to be in their way.

13. Can you hear my prayers for your help:
       are you listening to me when I cry out loud?

14. This is the time for you to come to my aid:
       I've never asked you before for any favours.

15. Why, God, why does this happen to me:
       is there no longer any justice in your sight?

16. Now I hear of the disasters that have happened
       to my friends:
       the cancer of my colleague
       and the car crash of my neighbour.

17. Did these things not occur before:
    or have I been too protected to notice it?

18. There's so much cruelty and evil around us:
    how can we survive when we're innocent victims?

19. Why, God, why does this happen to me:
    though plenty of others are suffering also?

20. I needed this time to think:
    never has the natural world been so important to me.

21. As things get better, there is still a nightmare:
    my life will never be the same, but at least I am alive.

22. I may have been beaten up, but I am not beaten down:
    now it's up to me to make a new life for myself.

23. What do I really want to do with my life:
    how can I make a contribution to my world?

24. Why, God, why did this happen to me:
    because you have changed my life for the better!

MAUNDY THURSDAY

Thursday is the day of the "Last" supper when Jesus in the John Gospel gave his disciples a new commandment ("mandatum" in Latin, shortened to "maundy").

The Thursday of Holy Week is "the day before Jesus died" on Good Friday; it was that night when he shared the "Last Supper" with the original cast. Sharing is at the heart of what the Gospel is about. "God so loved the world that he gave his only Son, so that everyone who believes should have eternal life." (John 3.16) Eternal life means sharing the life of God, because he wants to share his life with us. What an incredible gift! It is not something we have to work for (like the impressive Buddhist monks, keeping in mind hundreds of rules in order to earn a way to a higher life). God shares his Son with us. The Son shares himself with us – this is my body, and my blood.

But sharing isn't natural. We prefer to work hard for ourselves, and to keep what we have earned. You remember the story Jesus told about the servant who owed his master a million quid and was forgiven; then he put another servant in prison until he paid him back the fiver he owed! Sharing is part of the nature of God. It is not natural for me.

Perhaps that is the reason for the story of the foot washing in the John Gospel. It is done as an example to us. Jesus washed the disciples' feet, so that we might learn to wash one another's feet. Then we should be acting like Jesus, and like God. This is put in the place where the other 3 Gospels put the giving of bread and wine. When Jesus washes disciples' feet, he is doing the same thing as when he gives them bread and wine.

Communion means sharing. Having things in common. Not belonging to a society where some people get all the goodies and others have to do without, but rather serving one another and loving one another. If we do that, people will know we are disciples. It isn't what our world looks like, for sharing does not come naturally, and we do not believe in communism (whichever party happens to be in power). In the church, there should be just an inkling that things can be different, for communion means sharing. It doesn't always look like a meal, when all present are sharing things in common, and nobody is higher or better off than the rest. It was the same in Corinth. It didn't look like the communion at all! St Paul had to remind them what it was all like in the beginning. It is really a meal with a tablecloth, and we are all disciples around the table – some of us will deny our Lord and some will be weak, but we are all forgiven. None of us is Jesus ... or, rather, all of us are Jesus, because we all share his body and blood. For what we come to do is to share Jesus, to share God. That is what we mean by God; it is his nature always to be sharing himself with you and me.

> Was ever another command so obeyed? For century after century, spreading slowly to every continent and every country and among every race on earth, this action has been done, in every conceivable human circumstance, for every conceivable human need from infancy and before it to extreme old age and after it, from the pinnacles of earthly greatness to the refuge of fugitives in the caves and dens of the earth. Men have found no better thing than this to do for kings at their crowning and for criminals going to the scaffold; for armies in triumph or for a bride and bridegroom in a little country church; for the proclamation of a dogma or for a good crop of wheat; for the wisdom of the Parliament of a mighty nation or for a sick old woman afraid to die; for a schoolboy sitting an examination or for Columbus setting out to discover America; for the famine of whole provinces or for the soul of a dead lover; in thankfulness because my father did not die of pneumonia; for a village headman much tempted to return to fetish because the yams had failed; because the Turk was at the gates of Vienna; for the repentance of Margaret;

for the settlement of a strike; for a son for a barren woman; for Captain so-and-so, wounded and prisoner of war; while the lions roared in the nearby amphitheatre; on the beach at Dunkirk; while the hiss of scythes in the thick June grass came faintly through the windows of the church; tremulously, by an old monk on the fiftieth anniversary of his vows; furtively, by an exiled bishop who had hewn timber all day in a prison camp near Murmansk; gorgeously, for the canonisation of S. Joan of Arc – one could fill many pages with the reasons why men have done this, and not tell a hundredth part of them. And best of all, week by week and month by month, on a hundred thousand successive Sundays, faithfully, unfailingly, across all the parishes of Christendom, the pastors have done this just to make the *plebs sancta Dei* – the holy common people of God.

(Dom Gregory Dix: The Shape of the Liturgy: Dacre: London 1945. p.744)

PSALM

1. Jesus said, "I give you a new commandment:
      love one another as I have loved you;

2. then everyone will know you're my disciples:
      because of the care you show for one another."

3. Now, Lord, you have invited us to share in your supper:
      so we proclaim your death until you come again.

4. As you have washed our feet as the willing slave of all:
      so we wash one another's feet as servants of others.

5. The basin of water to refresh the weary:
      the towel to wipe the frustration of hard and bitter lives.

6. For you have given the Eucharist to your church:
      and the church you have given
      to the whole of the world.

7. The bread, which we break together:
      it's a sharing of your body, as we share the single loaf.

8. The cup of blessing that we bless:
      it's a sharing of your blood that's freely shed for us.

9. At the end we depart in disarray:
      what can I do, now you've left me all alone?

10. And yet, I'm not ever alone:
      for you are now inside me, I can live as part of your body.

GOOD FRIDAY

The story of Elie Wiesel is well known. It was in the Second World War death camp where a young boy of about his own age was to be hanged, with other men, and all Jews were to stand on parade and watch. The men died as soon as they were hanged, because of their body weight, but the boy took a long time to die, struggling with the rope round his neck. Someone muttered "Where is God now?" And Elie Wiesel says he heard a voice inside him say "There, hanging in front of you; that is where God is."

In the book of Exodus, God was on the mountain:

> "The people stayed away, while Moses approached the dark cloud,
> where God was." (Exodus 20.21)

So it is in a <u>dark</u> cloud, where God is? In the threat, the pain, the depression, the sadness, the dying – that is the place where God is? Most of us cannot take it. Most of us think God is supposed to take all that away, and make everything – all manner of thing— well. That is to say we feel that God should be making the darkness go away, removing the pain, and stopping people dying. The Gospel is perhaps rather about vanquishing darkness, rising through pain, and conquering death. Not that they are removed, but that they are overcome. So that Easter is not about "kissing it better" – not about "pie in the sky when you die" – nor is Christmas about "man shall live for ever more..." The Luke Gospel story of the two disciples walking on the road from Jerusalem to Emmaus was different from all that. Their experience was about the ability to understand that "the Son of Man must suffer..." It was about finding God in the difficulties, and the possibility that we might find ourselves being carried by God's footprints. Dennis Potter movingly said, in the interview just before his death, "You cannot know anything of God without suffering." It is a hard saying!

There is also an element of fearfulness around this dark cloud. Moses might have had enough courage to go there. Most of us would not be so stupid. (There is a view that some people who win awards for gallantry and courage are less thoughtful or imaginative than most! The rest of us would not be so stupid as to do that...) I am not courageous, anyway. It is easier to stay well away from God (if possible) and hide among other people. Let someone else go into the dark cloud.

PSALM

1. Behold the Cross displayed for all to see:
    the one who saves the world is hanging there.

2. They executed the awkward squad in the ancient world:
    we still believe in torture to show who's on top.

3. For the Cross of Christ was a gibbet not a decoration:
    an electric chair to deter not a trinket to attract!

4. The wise men came to know Christ by a star:
    the Cross is where we look to follow him today.

5. Unless I am burned away with the fire of love:
    consumed by the endless flames that cauterise me,

6. the only way I can learn to follow the Cross:
    must needs be through pain and loss,
    to be purged with tears.

7. For it wasn't the nails that kept Christ on his Cross:
    but the power of his love for us, that held him there.

8. So, Christ, print on my heart your love for me:
    your Cross has painted love in lively colours.

9. Behold the Cross displayed for all to see:
    hanging there is the one who saves the world.

10. On every one of my dyings shed your light:
    prove your love on your Cross and press me forward.

SATURDAY – the day before Easter

Traditionally, this is a quiet day, for thinking about what we have been following in the story, the dying of Jesus, for meditating on the mystery of it all. Of course, the pain and suffering remains a mystery. The Hebrew word for the dark cloud probably does not have the same connotation as the darkness of suffering, but is more to do with the secret or high place (and that is why God dwells there). For another kind of Easter experience is that of the local Mayor who said he had always thought that the world was full of bad people doing bad things. That is the impression we get from the media – for it is always the bad news that we hear and read (it's the bad things that are unusual; that is what news is!). But, after twelve months as a local Mayor, he had begun to realise that the world is actually full of good people doing good things.

So at least we can begin to see suffering and pain as part of life that demands our response. It calls from us the possibility of goodness. The mystery of the dark cloud is, at least partly, that there can be a silver lining. There is always the possibility of new life. Just as the dead looking tree in the spring bursts into new growth. So, even the worst moments of human experience, someone's illness or malice or death, can produce good. The very dawning of the new day is a resurrection. John Keble wrote that "every morning, our wakening and uprising prove" that God loves us. The scars of yesterday's hurt can prove a resurrection to us, as they did for Thomas. I think it was Dame Edith Sitwell who was explaining how a writer has to discipline herself to write something every day, whatever she was feeling like. The interviewer said, "That must be deadly." But she replied, "Oh yes – but there are many resurrections."

One of many telling, but short, phrases of the Gospel is in the John story of Easter. Peter and John, the two disciples, run to the tomb to see what the women were babbling about. John, being younger, got there first, and the story says, "yet went he not in." Perhaps there is a deep truth in those few words. Unless we are able somehow to "go in" to things, we will not be able to enter into the Easter experience for ourselves. It will remain a story, something that happened to someone else, or somewhere else, or it will remain an isolated event unconnected with the life Jesus lived and his revolutionary teaching. In the John story, fortunately, the disciple waited until Peter had gone in, and then followed him. It was he who then "saw and believed." Once we have been able to experience life from the inside, things can begin to look very different.

The very deadness of the natural world is itself a mystery, where there does not always seem much possibility of new life. Long after the volcanic eruption, there can be the startling brightness of colour on a new plant. Even broken relationships can bring some possibility of new life, perhaps forgiveness. "Can you drink of the cup that I drink?" asked Jesus, and assumed that we can. It is not a matter of finding glib answers, but of deepening the mystery.

PSALM

1. We adore you, Christ, and we bless you:
   because by your holy cross
   you have redeemed the world.

2. Saviour of the world, you've redeemed us by your passion:
   save us and help us now, we humbly pray.

3. Lord Jesus, you suffered on the cross alone:
    be close to those whose lonely suffering is hard to bear.

4. Your pain was undeserved:
    help innocent victims in their agonies.

5. For your cross fitted you so perfectly:
    grant us the strength to carry the crosses
    of this present moment.

6. Your hands and feet were nailed to the wood:
    preserve the faith and hope of those who are powerless.

EASTER EVE

After the death of Jesus, the celebration of his life still continues with the greatest Christian festival of Easter, the rising to life again of a dead man. The rebirth of the sun in the constellation of Aries mirrors the story of the rebirth of the Son who is the Lamb of God.

Easter happens in darkness, and brings the light of a new day, a different day. Good heavens, just look! During the night, someone has changed the world! The story goes on to when the disciples went back home, and so do we. We take the new day back home with us, the way that things look different, the way the world has changed. We take that back home with us, as disciples.

I had a friend who was a marvellous person, clever, good company, amusing. But he was not a believer. He didn't go to church, or at least he did go, but usually only at Christmas or Easter. That was the trouble, really. It was the stories of the great festivals that he found so difficult. And I have known plenty of priests (to say nothing of bishops) who have been heard to say quietly (I often wish they would speak it more openly!) that they do not believe the story of the Virgin Birth, or the story of the Empty Tomb, or life after death. Delightful people, all of them, only they do not believe. Or rather, it is not that they don't believe; it is that they do believe, but they are puzzled. What does resurrection mean? What does Easter mean?

Some people do know. Like the beloved disciple who got to the tomb and saw the cloths lying there, and believed. Some people today can still see and believe. They are lucky.

Others of us are just puzzled. Like Mary who got to the tomb in the darkness and said she didn't know what had happened. Like Peter who went straight into the tomb, but still he didn't understand. People like them today are still able to be disciples. Perhaps we shall never find the answers, for answers can sometimes be idols and not fit to be worshipped as God. God, perhaps, is always a question mark, always a mystery. The story of Easter begins in the darkness and mystery of dawn.

And it ends when disciples go home, puzzled or believing. Perhaps being a disciple of Jesus means what happens when we go home. It is that life, at home, that may be dead sometimes, or it may be risen, Christian life. We might spend our days puzzled or believing. That's not the bit that matters so much. More important that we go back home and live. For each morning is like Easter Day. It starts in darkness, then there is something new, for things have changed while we were not watching, and there is a new day in which to be a disciple.

PSALM

1. This is the night of your Passover, our God:
    when your faithful people were kept safe from destruction.

2. This the night you rescued Israel:
    freeing them from slavery through the Red Sea waters.

3. This is the moment that Christ broke free:
    the time of the conquest of the powers of hell.

4. On this night Jesus rose from the dead:
    so that all, both past and future, may share his triumph.

5. This night is the end of sinfulness:
    when all who believe are freed from slavery.

6. This is the time to heal all creation:
    for heaven and earth are joined in Jesus Christ.

7. So rejoice all powers of earth and heaven:
    all creatures of God sound the music of praise.

8. Christ has conquered, and all is new:
    the glory of God now fills the universe.

9. As the Paschal candle gives light to our world:
    we rejoice in Christ our light for ever more.

EASTER DAY

When I was at school, we used to play a game. A group of us would charge down the hill, or across the playground, shouting "Death or glory!" I never understood what it meant; though it was fun. I still don't understand what it meant. Presumably, we were pretending that either we would get clobbered by the other side, and that meant death; or else we would bash them up, and that meant glory.

Easter Day is about death and glory. And it doesn't involve anyone beating up the other side. Either we are all in this together, or you are on your own. It has sometimes been claimed that Easter is about me on my own, about life after death, for me. More hopefully, it is about all of us together, not just you and I and a few friends who happen to agree, but all people.

Pierre Teilhard de Chardin was a French Jesuit priest who died on Easter Day in 1955. He was struck by the idea of planet earth floating in space, though he never saw the pictures of earth taken from space, that we have seen since his day. The earth is a limited sphere. We cannot go on expanding forever. We can only learn to live on a finite planet. He thought of earth as folded in around itself, surrounded by a sort of spiritual stratosphere (what he called the "no-osphere"). And he thought we were all moving towards what he called the "omega point" – the end of the world, if you like. But he thought of it as a point when all humanity would be one, the Body of Christ. Sometimes, that vision seems wildly fantastic, because a post-modern world is flying off in different directions all at once. Yet we have got to where we are because of millions of others who have gone before us – grandparents, great grandparents, people in history books. And now that we are here, it's our responsibility to help things move on, towards an omega point, perhaps. When everyone will be part of the Body of Christ.

This kind of vision has taken a long time to appear, which makes you wonder how long it took for the story of Easter to evolve. Like so much else in the Gospel, this is a profound mystery, which will lead us into meditation for many of our fleeting years. Its importance is not so much about what happened on the second night after the crucifixion, but on what it means for us today. At Easter, we end the celebration of Jesus the human being, and begin the celebration of the Christ of God.

PSALM

1. God, you spoke to me first in my family:
   my early memories are of a group of three.

2. As I learned more of you,
   it was among a group of friends:
   just as Jesus chose others to continue in his trials,

3. the twelve to be with him together:
   his special friends were three from among them.

4. Sometimes I imagine you call me by myself:
   but you want to save me with my sisters and brothers.

5. It's in our relationships that you speak with us:
   in groups of your followers today
   we find your Spirit is with us;

6. my family and friends help me laugh at myself:
   those with whom I work can bring me joy
   and a sense of purpose.

7. Now I am my brother's keeper:
   we are all citizens of the world;

8. it is the nations you command us to teach:
   in the groups where we are, you want us as leaven.

9. Where two or three are gathered in each place
   there are you among us according to your promise;

10. we learn to co-operate in our endeavours:
    so we can recognise you in one another.

(Published in "Psalms for the Synod" by Parish & People)

EVERY STEP OF THE WAY

FIVE

TAKE-OFF

THE SEASON OF EASTER

Easter, like Christmas, has a time after the day itself to allow the message of the festival to sink in to our souls. "The Great 50 days" of Easter give time for contemplation of the central point of the Christian year. The "Paschal Candle" is lit at dawn on Easter Day and is extinguished after the reading of the Gospel on Ascension Day.

One night – admittedly, it was rather late – I frightened the living daylights out of myself. I had been reading a book about ancient history, the Pyramids, and why they were built so long ago, and whether there may have been some connection with people in South America, too. It was exploring the possibility that ancient people were trying to tell us something about the future. Because of the cataclysmic disasters that happened to them, and would happen again in 2012 ... on December 23rd, actually. I put the book down, and thought, "After all, thousands and thousands of years ago, they might easily have been a few years out." And then the church clock, which had not been working for some time, struck the hour!

Contemplating the ending of our world cuts you down to size a bit.

So why do we keep Easter? It always seems odd to me that we keep – religiously– – the 40 days of Lent, but we often ignore the 40 days of Easter. Which do you think should be the more important? The 40 days of Easter commemorate the story of Jesus being risen, and popping up among his disciples in the various stories we call his "resurrection appearances." Of course, there came a point when it was clear he was no longer popping up, so there had to be an end, an "ascension" story to allow Jesus finally to leave and go to heaven, where he rightly belongs.

"Go to father," she said, when I asked her to wed.
For she knew, that I knew that her father was dead.
And she knew, that I knew, what she meant when she said,
"Go to father!"

Hell is a bit hot to handle especially the blood-curdling kind of hell that's for bad people. I mean, hell, aren't we all bad sometimes? Surely God is able to deal with all of us, however bad we are? Though I don't pretend to know how that might work.

When it is said of Jesus that he was "going to the Father" it means he was going to heaven. Or rather, that being with his Father was the most important thing he could ever do.

The time between Easter Day and Ascension Day, counting both ends, is 40 days. And then, in another 10 days, is the celebration of Pentecost, another new beginning in the calendar, the giving of the gift of the "Spirit of Jesus" to his first followers. So we have a choice. We can celebrate the 40 days of Easter, or the 50 days of Easter. The word "Pentecost" simply means "the 50th day" (of Easter).

PSALM

1. Most people think of you as boring and distant:
       belief in God points to weakness
       or to problems in infancy.

2. But surely that can't be right:
       or, if it's sometimes true, it cannot be universal?

3. Either you don't exist and you aren't a god:
       or, if you're really God, you're vital to all of us.

4. Belief is the only thing that makes any sense:
       the alternatives don't add up to anything at all.

5. If I am simply alone, the aloneness is unbearable:
       if I am only a worm, why do I have such longings?

6. It's simpler to believe in you:
       I need to rest in something beyond myself.

7. Then you must be more important than just a god:
       you are critical for my confidence and for my future;

8.   I don't have to be out of the ordinary to believe in you:
          faith is part of what it means to be human.

9.   Nobody thinks it odd that I believe and trust in my partner:
          why should it be so strange to believe and trust in God?

10. Perhaps it's just religion that's controversial:
          faith and trust in you are crucial to life.

ROGATION - the fifth week of Easter

I knew a priest once – or I should rather say that I disliked one, once! Whenever he saw someone begging, he would disappear, and wait for one of us to get caught. Then he would magically reappear and ask us what we had done. "Sent him away? – Where's your Christian charity gone to then?" "Given him a quid? Now every beggar in the kingdom will come knocking on the door expecting money from you!" Whatever you had done, it was wrong. Well, that is one kind of Christianity, perhaps particularly associated with church people of some years ago. Perhaps there's a hangover from the past, but there is a particular kind of narrow Bible-punching faith that can sometimes give much the same impression today. There are still people who are attracted by that kind of simple faith and discipline, like the anxious parent who says, "Go and see what Jack's doing and tell him to stop it." It is a religion of sin and guilt. Some connect it particularly with the Nonconformist conscience or the Puritans. Dr Colin Morris, when President of Conference, used to say that people often regarded Methodists as the people who were against things – against drink, against gambling, against sex; if you enjoy it, we're against it! He said that people sometimes thought Methodists were people who believed in teetotal depravity!

There is another view, which is more modern, perhaps. The late Basil Hume said he had started off on the first way, but began to look around for what is good in the world instead. Taking the world as a good place doesn't mean that I am not Puritanical about some things, of course – pornography, exploitation, or violence, for example! But there is quite a movement of learning to find what is good and becoming more in touch with it, learning how to grow by valuing, affirming, cherishing other people and myself. Before I can deny myself, I am likely to need the assurance of love from God and my family, and those I work with, too.– "Nothing can separate us from the love of God..." (Romans 8.39). But we do need to be reminded of the fact frequently!
If this is a better way than an emphasis on sin and guilt, then at least it makes it respectable to ask God for things for myself and for others. Rogationtide is part of the rural round of festivals and celebrations that used to be, and still is, such

an important part of country life. Asking for God's blessing on the crops of the new season, and looking forward to a good harvest. For Pentecost was itself a festival of the wheat harvest, one of the pilgrim festivals of the old covenant of Israel. Rogation was often a time of processions, too, and in the days before printed maps there was sometimes a solemn "beating of the bounds" with sticks of willow, to impress upon everyone just where the boundaries were. Children in particular were expected to learn the boundaries, and were sometimes also beaten with the sticks, or bumped on the boundary lines, to help their memory! The religious ceremony was fasting and the singing of litanies, abolished in the time of Elizabeth I, and now rarely used anywhere. All we have left are the prayers for the welfare of all people, and especially for the success of the coming harvest.

PSALM

1. There are times when believing is easy:
   when God speaks clearly for me to hear;

2. beforehand, you are often silent:
   while I ask for help, and there is none.

3. My new job is arranged; it seems to be right:
   the letter will confirm the decision in due course,

4. but, in the post, it is delayed too long:
   and another request is received to take its place.

5. So God makes clear the way:
   you prepare my path before me.

6. Disaster strikes! I might have been in that car:
   there, but for the grace of God, go I.

7. In smaller ways, there seem to be signs:
   pointing to new ideas, giving me a jolt.

8. So God makes clear the way:
   you prepare my path before me.

9. It seems, when all goes well, a hand is guiding:
   even when troubles come,
   there often seems some reason.

10. In looking back, I can see God's hand:
    though the future is still misty and unsure.

11. So God makes clear the way:
    you prepare my path before me,

ASCENSION

Ending the 40 days of Easter, Ascension Day always falls on a Thursday. Not, therefore, a good day to celebrate (unless you are part of a religious foundation, like a school or a convent, perhaps), so it is often postponed to the Sunday after. There is also another day later on, kept as the festival of "Christ the King" which is on the last Sunday of the year, the Sunday before Advent. For it has always been the genius of Christianity to link together the pre-Easter Jesus, the human being, from Nazareth, with the post-Easter Christ, the king and God.

There are two feelings I have about Ascensiontide. First, that this is the most marvellous part of the Christian year – I believe in it. Secondly, that the story of the Ascension is about the most fairy-tale bit of the whole story, and I can't believe a word of it, literally.

For one thing, the story of the Ascension is only found, in its traditional form, in the writing of St Luke. Older versions seem to assume that Jesus was raised and exalted by God, as if they were both the same thing. Ascension is only another part of the story of Easter, Christ is risen. You can't take stories about sitting on thrones, especially when they are on the right hand side of someone else, literally. Even the most red-necked fundamentalist of them all can't believe Jesus is actually sitting up there somewhere above the clouds?

On the other hand, the idea of a human being as King of the universe is always *gripping*, and people down the centuries have been taken with the idea, so that "Christ the King" is sometimes a dedication for a church, and certainly the theme for at least one Sunday in the Year, even if it is the last. Perhaps we first come across the picture of Christ as King when we find him as our personal saviour, who speaks to me in the quiet of my heart, and whose words to me nobody else can hear – the king of my private life. But that is never enough for mature disciples. Christ must also be king of our public life and of our whole world. As Hendrik Kraemer, the Dutch layman and author of *A Theology of the Laity*, used to say, every Christian needs at least two conversions: first to Christ, and then to the world!

We may each understand the kingship of Christ in different ways. Jesus could not explain it, so he kept telling stories, apparently. We can't explain it, so we keep doing this, in remembrance of him.

There are two other things, which are true of any great event in our lives. It is usually a new beginning and also a kind of an ending, too. A marriage may be the beginning of a new life together, but it also represents the ending of single life, whatever that means to you. Ascension is just like that. There had to be an ending of the earthly life of Jesus, including his risen life. True, Saint Paul thought he had seen the risen Christ on earth – on the way to Damascus, actually. But even he recognised that he was doing a bit of special pleading. Many people meet the risen Christ today, too. But it isn't quite the same as for the first disciples who knew him. Ascension was when Jesus said, now I have gone; it's over to you. Ending is not easy. "Parting is such sweet sorrow..." except for those times when it isn't sweet at all! We all know how very hard it can be to say "goodbye," and how we say "Well, goodbye then," several times before we manage finally to leave. How difficult it is to end a telephone conversation. Yet endings are vital. We have to move on. Clinging to the past, like clinging to the risen Christ, doesn't help ("Noli me tangere" spoken to Mary Magdalen in the garden, is usually said to mean, "don't keep on clinging on to me."). Ending things is vital. It is part of life.

Ascension is also a new beginning. Christ is going up, to be king, to be God. If Christianity is a religion of incarnation (which means that God came to be with us as a human being), Ascension means that a man has gone to be part of God (which means we have our representative in heaven, our man in God). Ascension begins a whole new way of thinking. Beginning things is often thought to be all wonderful. But it also can lead us into difficulties, hard work, changing our attitudes, finding our way around all over again. Beginning may be terrific, but tomorrow morning we have to change the nappies, get lost in a strange place, or be ignored as a mere newcomer. After the honeymoon, things get harder! Christians are not too good at taking the Ascension on board. It is quite hard to know that Christ is King and that all will be well.

Perhaps it is because we still think of it as an ending. Beginnings and endings can make us nervous, on edge. It's a bit like the time between VE and VJ Day – World War 2 was over at the Victory in Europe, but there was still a battle to be faced before the Victory in Japan. Christ is King, but I still have to live my life. We all have to wait for Pentecost to happen.

PSALM

1. Teach me, God, to see life backwards:
     to praise you for everything I've learned.

2. A sunset redeems the dullest day:
     I can look back from today in brilliant technicolour;

3. for you help me see glory in ordinary things:
     to feel significance in daily living -

4. as the taste of food in the mouth removes
     pangs of hunger:
     the experience I've gained so far
     takes the labour out of learning.

5. Teach me, God, to find you backwards:
     for treating you as history doesn't seem to work out!

6. Early Christians found you in Antioch:
     looking back they saw Jesus your Son
     as risen and ascended;

7. later on, they wrote down his story:
     gospel writers had messages to share -

8. as the prism that separates fractured light:
     the dazzling truth of God shines through my past.

9. In looking back from today I see flashes of presence:
     we cannot expect to see you, by being in front of you -

10. just as Moses was asking to see your glory:
      but was only able to bear to look at your back.

11. If it's in looking backwards I can see more colour:
      help me also look forward in hope -

12. as Moses climbed the mountain into cloud:
      I can travel from childish certainties to find your mystery.

PENTECOST

This is a festival of light, at the brightest time of the day and in the middle of the summer with the sun at its highest. For the light of God's Spirit is brighter than the sun at its brightest. A fire settled on each of the disciples in their Upper Room. They became new people, fired with courage and enthusiasm. Sometimes called the birthday of the Church, to represent the breaking out of the newly found mission.

When Jesus left this earth (to paraphrase words of Austin Farrer in a sermon on Pentecost Fire), he left behind two things. One was seen, and one was unseen. He left behind his Spirit and he left the Communion service; the Holy Spirit and the Holy Communion. So, when God gave the gift of his Spirit to the disciples at Pentecost, he gave it in two forms – one was seen and one was unseen, or perhaps one was felt and one was un-felt. The gift is unseen, first of all:

> For the fruit of the Spirit is love, joy, peace, patience, kindness, gentleness, fidelity and self control. (Gal. 5.22)

You cannot see qualities like that, or at least you can't see the gift of the Spirit that produces those fruits. By definition, you might think, the gift of God's Spirit is (like God) unseen. Now some Christians would argue with you about it. They might say that they need to know who is Spirit-filled and who is not yet converted. But you may be right to say the gift of Holy Spirit is spiritual not visible. It shows itself in our faces, maybe. Though preachers do tend to say that the average congregation does not look very spirit-filled – we prefer to keep our feelings to ourselves! After all, church is an objective thing. We come to worship God, but we don't expect to feel very much, or to see any angels. It is a commitment, a duty, and a determination to carry on believing, even against all the odds. That is what the word "liturgy" means. Clergy are supposed to say the daily offices. That is their duty. To be able to carry on with the commitment and not to give up. That is the Spirit at work. But you cannot see it.

The Pentecost gift of Holy Spirit was also something quite, quite visible. A close encounter of the first kind means to see an Unidentified Flying Object; a close encounter of the second kind means to show signs of your meeting, with burns or scorch marks; but a close encounter of the third kind means actually to meet ET, and the encounter changes you. It is not just a question of knowing about the Spirit, not just going to church, not just doing your duty. It is being touched and encountered by God. As, one evening in May, John Wesley said his "heart was strangely warmed." It may happen to you now. For some people, it happens only once in a lifetime. For others, it can happen several times. It is not possible to organise it, nor simply to make it happen when you want to. But you can certainly see it, or feel it.

PSALM

1. "Be strong and full of courage:
      for God is with you wherever you go."

2. The Spirit of God strengthens my hand:
      you make us bolder in our work together.

3. For in us all is the breath of life:
      you give true life to the people of God.

4. Come, Holy Spirit, as the mighty wind:
      as on the face of the waters at creation.

5. Give us your spirit of wisdom and understanding:
      the strength of good counsel and inner confidence;

6. bring us knowledge and heavenly insight:
      that we may delight in the worship of God.

7. In you we find ourselves made whole:
      your healing power is here for us when we need it.

8. Come, Holy Spirit, as the gentle dove:
      as you appeared to Jesus at the river of Jordan.

9. You bring love and joy and peace:
      the gifts of kindness, patience and goodness,

10. in you is the promise of faithfulness:
      the quality of real humility and self-control.

11. We feel your prophetic inspiration:
      our words can be clearer when we wait on you.

12. Come, Holy Spirit, as flames of fire:
      as you came to the twelve apostles at Pentecost.

13. We wait for your stirring power:
      my heart is wonderfully warmed
      by your comforting presence.

14. Your fire burns away the injustice of the world:
      the uselessness of evil you consume like kindling wood.

15. Then we may share your gifts:
      in serving one another we are living in your love.

16. Come, Holy Spirit, as the bond of love:
      for you join the Father and the Son as one God in unity.

17. The whole love of God has been poured in our hearts:
      through you, Holy Spirit, as you're given to us.

EVERY STEP OF THE WAY

PART THREE

SIX

LANDING

INTRODUCTION

The second part of the year is quite different from what has gone before, though it does start with some major festivals. The colour of the season is mostly green, which gives it a feeling of growth and a sort of straightforwardness. The "Sundays after Trinity" take up most of the year, and there are those who feel they provide just a boring series of "ordinary time" in the calendar (the fifth Sunday is followed by the sixth Sunday, and on, and on). But the reason for this second part of the year is to allow us to experience the second part of living, the breathing out. After Pentecost, the so-called "birthday of the Church," this is the time to follow the story of Christian people, those who follow the Way. Having taken a journey in the steps of Jesus, now we take our own faltering steps, following him.

The story of the Lord of the Rings is also a story of a journey. That is a long and hazardous journey to destroy the evil power of the ring, which takes over anyone who wears it. Frodo Baggins of Bag End has inherited the ring, and it is his task to destroy it. He takes with him on the journey his faithful servant, Sam Gamgee. They go to the limits of Sam's knowledge, the edge of The Shire. And, at this point, Frodo tells Sam he really needn't come any further. It has become clear that the journey is going to be frightening and dangerous. He has done his master a good turn by helping him start on his way. But now he should go back home, and leave Frodo to complete the task, which is rightly his alone. But Sam, surprisingly, resists.

> I don't know how to say it, but after last night I feel different. I seem to see ahead, in a kind of way. I know we are going to take a very long road, into darkness; but I know I can't turn back. It isn't to see Elves now, nor dragons, nor mountains, that I want - I don't rightly know what I want: but I have something to do before the end, and it lies ahead, not in the Shire. I must see it through, sir, if you understand me.
> (Lord of the Rings. JRR Tolkein. London, Book Club Associates. 1971 p.100)

Every Step of the Way

That is, for me, one of the classic expressions of the quest. Like King Arthur and the stories of the Holy Grail, and like so many novels and tales, we are aware of the journey which has to be completed, and which we cannot delegate to someone else. But this example is crucially not about saints, poets, kings, bishops or knights, but about the servants, those who need not be involved and who nevertheless opt for the road they have to take.

This second part of the year, too, has its introduction and its conclusion. It ends with the Kingdom Season (a way of preparing us for Advent when the year begins again), the four Sundays before Advent, ending with the festival of Christ the King. But, as its introduction, one week after Pentecost there is the festival of the Trinity in May or June. Nothing like beginning this journey of faith at the deep end! We begin with God, and the being of God, God as the Trinity of Persons, Father, Son and Holy Spirit.

PSALM

1. God you are truth, and I need to find the truth:
    I want to face things as they really are;

2. you are love, and you come to meet us:
    we are caught up in your love that embraces everything.

3. For your goodness brings us so much to enjoy:
    the initiative comes from the other side;

4. your glory I see in other people:
    in music and art, in silence and beauty,
    your grace shines bright.

5. This real world offers so much from you:
    there is promise of good in all things,

6. help me see and enjoy more and more of it:
    so I can share in the sharing of God.

7. For I believe that God is:
    that is all there is to be said.

8. *God is as Jesus shows us:*
    and therefore there is hope.

9. The story of the Bible reveals your wonders:
    through its patterns I learn of your goodness.

10. In Jesus I meet your presence:
    I encounter your call to me, as I read your word.

11. So I come to know you as God:
     you are the power of justice, love and holiness.

12. But all do not share in this faith:
     for God is not revealed to us all
     without shadow of doubting,

13. we still look for everything to be made clear:
     in the future, your kingdom will come in its fullness.

14. So shall we believe that God is:
     that will be all we need to affirm.

15. *God is as Jesus shows us:*
     and therefore there is hope.

16. God the Father is greater than great:
     you are before and beyond everything that is.

17. God the Son is more loving than love:
     you are with us and beside us in all our relationships.

18. The Spirit is God closer than close:
     you are in us and around us in everything that happens.

19. In all, you are God of the universe:
     the same God, revealing your love in all the earth.

20. Yet the universe is interpreted by science:
     how can we have faith in the midst of randomness? -

21. and religion is contradicted by religion:
     how can we find love in the fight for orthodoxy?

22. Perhaps this God is committed to risk:
     in Jesus you were open to suffering love,

23. so you are with me in all that befalls me:
     in my confusion I can follow your lead.

24. I believe that you are here:
     that is all I need to know.

25. *You are always at my side:*
     so the struggle of life is worth it.

26. Pictures from space show our planet is limited:
     if we waste our resources this world cannot survive.

27. Television shows us our peoples are divided:
     barbed wire keeps the affluent away from the poor.

28. Under threat of nuclear destruction what will our God do:
    will you stop us exploding the earth
    by working a miracle?

29. Or perhaps you will save us with a miracle of patience:
    as more of us are growing older,
    we may learn to be more tolerant?

30. So the pressures around us may lead us to hope:
    under God there is always time,
    another five minutes to midnight;

31. while love and justice can grow with endurance:
    for you share our dreams of future possibilities.

32. We believe that God is:
    that is all we need to affirm.

33. *God is always on our side:*
    so the struggle of life is worth it.

34. To refuse to love is to give way to apathy:
    if people do not care, no improvement is possible.

35. But there's no need to despair of everything:
    we can always find glimpses of glory.

36. We can learn to follow what light we have:
    and earnestly pray for more.

37. Anything we do is a risk:
    but women and men are of infinite worth,

38. for loving each other is possible, humanity can flourish:
    in spite of our everyday problems, all our living is worth it!

39. We believe that God is:
    that is all we need to say.

40. *God is as Jesus shows us:*
    and therefore there is hope.

TRINITY

So what is God the Holy Trinity? God may be a great mystery, but we love to make a divine mess of philosophical puzzles about it! Yet all of us have had the experience of, say, working with a colleague, someone whom we feel we know quite well. Then the family comes to meet them at the end of a day at work, and we suddenly see them as a father or mother too. It almost seems as if they become a different person, and one we hardly know at all. I suppose that may be one way of trying to make some sense of God as our creator, as our friend and Master, and as the divine Spirit within each of us.

PSALM

1.   You are God and I trust in you:
        for you are my friend and I meet you in other people.

2.   You are worth all that I can give:
        you give worth to everything that exists;

3.   though everything needs to be changed and redeemed:
        you will challenge and re-create all we do and are.

4.   You are my master and my creator:
        you are my loving father and my strong protector.

5.   You are my mother and my supporter:
        my caring sister and my close companion.

6.   You are my power and my comfort:
        my heartbeat and my continuing sustenance.

7.   Stay beside me whatever may happen:
        my maker, my shaker, and my renewer,

8.   be at my side in times of anguish:
        as power, possibility and presence,

9.   remain in me through all the good that comes:
        with your life and hope and glory.

TRINITY SUNDAY

I have always had difficulty with modern art. There was a Picasso exhibition at the Tate Gallery in London (Tate Britain as it now is) many years ago, and I enjoyed it, although it was extremely crowded and I didn't buy the catalogue as it was so very expensive. I particularly enjoyed one picture there. It was clearly an industrial scene, with buildings at all angles and power lines across the picture. Eventually, I managed to sneak a look at someone else's catalogue where it gave the title, "Nude with violin." Obviously, pictures can be misleading! So how would you fare if you were trying to draw a picture of God? When you ask small children to do it, they will often draw a big king sitting on a throne, or an old man looking a bit like Father Christmas with a long beard. How *do* you picture God?

We try more often to worship God. It is not so easy to do that, either, because the pictures get in the way. I used to say, "because the <u>words</u> get in the way." But the pictures are difficult, too. How can we possibly picture God? Nowadays, our difficulties start when we begin to think of a person. Is God a Father? So then he must be a man, and more and more people therefore want to speak of God as female as well. Some people think that's why many Christians regard Mary as so important, almost a fourth member of the Trinity, making certain there is really a woman in there somewhere, as well! Or perhaps God the Holy Spirit should be regarded as female? Or perhaps this does not matter to you ... yet! For, it seems, these days, as if it's only a matter of time before we find we are not helped by the pictures in our head, or (to change the metaphor) we find that our ears have popped and some words cannot be used without question any longer. Perhaps you can find a picture that is more about personal power and influence, rather than merely <u>a</u> person. If so, does your God speak to you or call you by name? Can you pray to power or influence, however personal they may be? Or, if you cannot easily see or hear God, can you sense him or her in any way at all (by touch or smell or taste)?

We try to worship God, but how can we meet God? Or rather, how can God meet us? For our worship has to be a response, on our part, to a God who has already approached us, and met us, not necessarily today, but at some time. God has come close to you, and now you are compelled to worship.

Some people find that God meets us through our experiences, especially in new places. Like the person who went to India for the first time and it spoke to her so powerfully that she said it felt as if God had met her there. Or the man who had been on holiday to Africa, and was compelled to go back again, and again. For some of us, God meets us in other people – the things they say, the kind of people they are, the way they care for us, or their personal qualities of courage, for example. So God can come close to us through other persons and other places. Some of us find an experience of God through our closeness to one person in particular. The fact that someone else loves you can be about the most powerful experience in your life. When someone else is prepared to accept you as you are, to put up with you in the same house, as your parent, child, partner. That may be why the family is so important to many of us, because it is where we find acceptance and therefore strength and confidence. It is in the same sort of way that we find God "speaking" to us, with acceptance and love.

Others find God in the experience of meeting Jesus again, in the words of the Gospels or the stories of faith, and in the Jesus who meets us in the Holy

Communion, through the breaking of the bread, which is his body. At least images are possible here. Jesus was most certainly a man! (Yet the pictures we have been brought up with are very odd - the television actor with funny clothes, the voice of an American or English man speaking Shakespearean seventeenth century words from the King James version of the Gospels, or a blue-eyed Victorian portrait which is not middle-eastern at all.) At least, it is easier to feel I can have some sort of relationship with a human being, like myself (even if he was also very unlike me). If Jesus is also God, then I can begin to have some sort of a picture.

PSALM

1.   Before all things began, the Word was there:
        one Word of life already, at the world's creation;

2.   for what God was, the Word was also:
        rooted and grounded in love, for God is love.

3.   All creation was made by the Word of God:
        all love was shown by God, and by that Word on earth,

4.   for through him, God spoke to us:
        and, by his Word, God said, "I love you".

5.   The Spirit was there already when all things were created:
        your breath moved over the mists at the world's
        beginning;

6.   since that Spirit is the Spirit of love:
        inspiring and encouraging us all, you are in us always.

7.   So Creator and Spirit are one:
        you've been here since the beginning,
        and you're also with us,

8.   in loving and creating you are at work:
        your love is in us now, through Word and Spirit.

CORPUS CHRISTI – Thursday after Trinity Sunday

At a theological college, or on a training course, people are expected to read a lot of books. Some of them are boring, and you try not to open those; some of them are all right and you skip through bits of those; but some of them get to you. The first time I had that experience, I remember thinking, "But I've never heard any of this before; it must be a very new book." So I looked at the front and saw it was written in the year that I was born. Yet I was not aware that anyone had even suggested the ideas to me before. I felt quite angry.

Another of those books that got to me was one about Easter that came as a revelation to me. We are brought up with the Protestant idea that the Communion service is a remembering of the death of Jesus of Nazareth, and we are saved because he died for us, to remove our sinfulness and guilt, so that we can stand up and be real human beings. That was the teaching of St Paul. It is there in the Luke Gospel, because Luke was a disciple and friend of Paul, and may perhaps have been his doctor. But there is another story that has also got into the Luke Gospel, and it does not seem to come from Paul. That is the story of the two disciples walking back home after the festival, on the road from Jerusalem. It is often said that this is the most beautiful story in the Gospels. It is certainly most beautifully crafted and written, wherever it comes from originally (was it perhaps conceived by the Gospel writer?).

I am struck by how the disciples seem not to have understood the resurrection very quickly – the change seems to come at Pentecost, after 50 days (in other words, a very long time), not on Easter Day. What changed the disciples from frightened followers, who locked themselves into a Jerusalem upstairs room, into missionaries not afraid to be beaten or killed for their beliefs, was the risen Christ. But it took them some little time to take the change on board. It takes some of us more like a lifetime! Even then, I am not sure that I can get all that far along the road. The resurrection of Jesus is not so simple as it sounds in the Easter Day stories. That is why we celebrate them for the 40 days of Easter up to Ascension Day. The reason for this is obvious, if you think about it.

Jesus used to meet with the disciples to eat. Jews still have important family meals, when no member of the family would dream of being absent (unlike many non-Jewish families today!). Jesus did the same, and the Passover meal is one supreme example (if that is what they were doing in the Upper Room on Maundy Thursday). After Easter, the disciples still had to eat, and they tried to do the same as they had done while Jesus was alive. They said grace and broke the bread.

And that's when it happened.

It is, of course, difficult to describe, but somehow it seemed almost as if Jesus had not died. It became quite clear to them that he was very much alive, when they ate their meal together. It was the breaking of the bread that did it. So the early disciples found that, when they met to eat together, Jesus was there too, just as he had always been, except that they couldn't keep him there.

Have you ever felt like that, too? As if Christ were beside you in the room, perhaps in church or maybe in other places too, except that you can't keep him there? Part of the skill of praying is the prolonging of that moment of closeness or presence. And that is perhaps what our Communion service is about, as well, a re-membering of the resurrection of Jesus the Christ. That is why we do it on Sunday mornings, and not on Friday afternoons. The Eucharist is not so much to remember the death of Jesus, but to celebrate his presence with us now. We do this not just in a church, but in our own private times of prayer, or our family meals or activities with other people. But that's why the Eucharist is particularly important, for we are re-membering, putting together again, the body of Christ, in remembrance of him.

That is why there is this festival of Corpus Christi, the body of Christ, on the first available Thursday after Easter, pointing back to the Thursday immediately before Easter (Maundy Thursday) the commemoration of the Last Supper. It is the first available Thursday because all the other Thursdays are part of the festive days of Easter or Ascension or Pentecost, which have their own place in the calendar. But this day is just an ordinary day, after Trinity Sunday. Thomas Aquinas it was, first of all, who wrote special services for this day. It came to be thought of as foreign to many Protestant Christians, to say nothing of non-church people, for the Eucharist is, by definition, an occasion for the initiated, for the insiders. Corpus Christi also means the body of Christians.

PSALM

1. The Lord is here - let all mortal flesh keep silence:
   humanity must be humble in the presence of God.

2. For Christ is risen and now is with us always:
   his real presence is assured because of Easter.

3. Lord, your sacrament is wonderful
   beyond our understanding:
   you make yourself known to us in the breaking of bread.

4. Yet you appear so often in ordinary people and places:
   even disciples don't always recognise you.

5. This bread is a sign of our daily work:
   the toil of a breadwinner who provides for the family;

6. our food must needs be broken before we can digest it:
   you're daily broken in us so you can be with us.

7. This wine is a sign of suffering:
    the shedding of blood for the sake of others;

8. all our lesser sacrifices are gathered up in your Cross:
    as willingly we accept this cup of your promise.

9. You come close to us in full communion:
    just as once you came in flesh
    and will come in your Kingdom.

10. As I can see you in this sacrament:
    so I know you are with me always from day to day.

11. You have given your body and blood for me:
    now you are within me and part of me forever.

12. As we eat at the table you are here:
    when we are together in your name
    there are you among us.

EVERY STEP OF THE WAY

SEVEN

PRAYER

GOD OF THE PROPHETS

Elijah was a prophet, and the stories about him starting in the First Book of the Kings are brilliant and bloodthirsty. I have never actually used them as bedtime stories for children, but they are not bad for that! One of my teachers did read them to us, and obviously enjoyed them immensely himself. I remember sitting at my desk, at the age of twelve, interested and alert, aware that our classroom was above an old dungeon in a castle, and beneath the floor was a trap-door...

What is a prophet? It is a person who can look at the ordinary daily events of life around us, and see in them the work of God.

In ancient times, people actually got paid for doing that. It was a job, a career. Nowadays it may be a vocation, but not often a profession. The paid prophet interpreted to the clan, to kings making decisions or generals about to go into battle, to those thinking of marriage or the parents of the newly born, what those signs meant for them. The signs might have been the innards of an animal sacrificed for the purpose, or the cards, or their dreams. What they meant for them could be that they would be successful, or that they would fail, that they would marry the right person or lose the battle, that they would prosper or that they would be dead by this time tomorrow. It was a matter of life or death. Obviously there is good money to be had by someone who knows what the future holds. Some people still earn a living from it, even if it is not a mainstream profession as it once was, and even fewer now see it as a vocation. Elijah was, presumably, not paid by King Ahab – the person who addressed him with the words, "Have you found me out, my enemy?" There was a continuing prophetic tradition in the Bible, leading on to Jeremiah, Amos and others, who operated as a sort of political opposition. Queen Jezebel certainly needed an opposition.

So do we. We call it "whistle-blowing" and there is a clear need for prophecy at every level in our society, too. Sometimes, it can be no less dramatic than it was for Jezebel! But, most of the time, it is a far more mundane business. In that sense, we are all called to be prophets, too

First, by earning the right to be listened to. We are all of us expected to have a view, sometimes, and to be able to express it in our family, in our work place, or at the street corner.

Secondly by being a person of prayer, who listens to God and to other people, reflecting on your own experience and what you think seems to be being said. Listening is not a simple matter. There is plenty about it in the Bible, where there are warnings about those who can hear but do not listen! To remind me of it, I have a text in my study, which reads:

"I know that you believe
you understand what I said,
but I'm not sure you realise that
what you heard is not what I meant."

A prophet today is someone who can really listen and reflect on what is happening. It means being a listener to God and to other people. All of us are called to do that.

The young are called; the elderly are called. There is no retirement from the Christian pilgrimage. The beautiful are called, and also the unlovely. The sick are called as well as the healthy and the energetic. Activists are called and also quiet people. We are called regardless of our intellectual abilities or our formal education. We are called regardless of our race or nationality or social class.

Women are called, and men are called. The poor are called, and perhaps the Church of England has begun to understand the gifts which they have, and what we may learn from them. Yet God 'has no favourites' and equally calls to discipleship the rich and the comfortable.

We are all called no matter what our occupations may be. There is no special status in the Kingdom for those in 'top jobs' or with 'important responsibilities'. Cleaners and car dealers are called just as much as professors and lawyers and missionary nurses. And unemployed people and redundant people and 'unemployable' people are called just like everybody else. Our human dignity does not depend on having a job.
Nor does our calling – our vocation – depend on any kind of *ordination*. There are still many deep controversies about what

ordination may signify, in many Churches and within our own Church of England. But it certainly does not indicate any special 'grade' of Christian, more holy than the laity. And for everybody, bishops, priests and laity together, the great sacrament of our common calling is our baptism, which signifies our glorious new life in Christ.

This New Testament teaching about vocation has been rediscovered in the last thirty years by Christians of many different denominations, Catholics and Protestants alike. We can thank God that it is now strongly affirmed by many members of the Church of England, whether of high or low persuasion.

What is more, this call comes to us all, for all of our days and years, and for all of our activities.

Church of England Report "All Are Called" CIO 1985   *(now out of print)*

PSALM

1. When I was not expecting it, you called me, my God:
   I hear you in a moment of time,
   when I'm doing something else.

2. At the corner of a dried up field there's an open gate:
   helping me find new pathways, leading me on.

3. Christ, you have opened for me the gate of glory:
   so I can find greater wonders in your wonderful world;

4. yet un-trodden paths can be dark and frightening:
   frontiers are places of conflict and confusion.

5. Spirit, help me to discern the way I should go:
   how else can I be sure that I've found the open door?

6. At times you will close the door I thought I'd found:
   be with me and support me then, when I feel most alone.

7. Help me learn to expect you in new and surprising places:
   to look for your truthful word
   in the judgements of others;

8. when those seem wrong to me, help me to learn:
   when they seem right, keep me from pride!

THE LUKE GOSPEL

I have always had a problem about sin. That is because I do not see myself as someone who was once a great sinner, who had a wonderful experience of conversion at the age of 25, despised my former life and changed direction completely, since when my life has been entirely Christian. I do not see myself as someone like, say, Saint Francis. Perhaps that kind of story is only for saints, since most of us are much more mixed up than that!

But I do not have such a problem about love. Most of us do not love ourselves very much, we are full of guilt, we do not like how we look, and spend great effort in trying to make ourselves into something we are not. Indeed, some of us are not aware of having been loved when we were just kids.

One of the intriguing things about the Luke Gospel is its attitude to people who are not Jews. God loves all people ... you don't have to be a Jew to be a Christian. And, in the non-Jewish world of his day, an attitude to women which is more positive than might be expected. (Sometimes I dream about whether, as in the case of George Eliot or the Bronte sisters, Luke might have been a *nom de plume* for a woman?) Luke tells us about the women disciples, well-off women, able to afford expensive oils and spend them on Jesus, able to house and feed him and his 12 disciples. And there were numerous women. Why do we think of 12 men as the only disciples? It sounds as if there are in this story many more than 12 women, as well!

There is the story of the woman who poured expensive ointment on Jesus's head and washed his feet with her tears. Whenever I have seen it portrayed, it comes out as blatantly sexual. I wonder if that is a modern interpretation of what was more normal in a first century hot country? The "immoral" woman is usually equated with a prostitute (who may not have been considered quite that immoral, then, just a person to be despised?). She certainly had a reputation. The Luke Gospel makes the point that Jesus is someone who takes people as they are, rather than one who deals with people depending on their class. This woman was being valued and loved, and she cried. The reaction of the Pharisees, in Luke's story, is "If Jesus were a prophet, he'd know what sort of person this woman is." Part of my job has often been trying to discern 'what sort of person' this is. We all spend our lives categorising people. We could hardly live without doing it. It can be destructive when we stereotype other people, judging them. So the word "pharisaic" has come to mean being snobbish, looking down on others, showing that our standards are so much better than theirs are (when they are not!).

The response of Jesus, according to Luke, is to ask about love. If the woman was actually a prostitute that may have had another twist; he was perhaps saying this is not about making love, but about love. Luke was trying to show that the real Jew, the Pharisee, showed little love, while the immoral woman was showing great love. Perhaps that was because Jesus had made her feel valued, not rejected. This Gospel is saying that God values you, even if you are not a Jew, a man, a Pharisee, a vicar or a saint.

Francis Dewar, writing about the qualities of Christian ministry, begins by offering his view of the basic qualities of Christian maturity, anyway. He thinks they can be reduced to two: "groundedness in God and a good enough sense of your own worth."

> "By groundedness in God I mean living your life in the conscious awareness that he is the source and goal of your life; that all that you are is from him, that you are his creation, and that your deepest longing is for him; that you are deeply loved, more than by any human being, and infinitely more than you can love yourself, and that his love reaches even to the farthest and darkest corners of your personality; that you are a treasure of infinite worth, to be his gift to others in what you do."
> (Francis Dewar, *Called or Collared?* SPCK 1991, p. 96)

He explains what he means by "a good enough sense of your own worth" like this:
> "Most of us harbour deep within us the opposite of this. We lack a sense of worth or of value and expend a good deal of energy trying to compensate for that. We try and bolster our own low self-esteem by status-seeking or by running other people down in one way or another, and 'all because [we] cannot get on with [ourselves] and have not the slightest faith that anything useful could ever come out of [our] own souls' (C.G. Jung, *Dreams*, Ark Paperbacks 1985, p. 175). Learning self-acceptance is admittedly a life-long task for most of us, which is why I say that what is required is a *good enough* sense of your own worth."   (op.cit. p.98)

PSALM

1. You, my God, are the strength of my life:
    you've been my companion through everything.

2. Before I was born, you were there:
    you were present in the love of my parents.

3. I can't understand my own beginning:
    for you are the mystery that's in all creating;

4. you formed me from generations before me:
    as a unique gift, you made me what I am.

5. Yet I'm always in the middle of conflicts:
    it feels as if the war goes on inside me;

6. just as the world is wonderful and terrible:
    and you are on both sides all the time!

7. In the darkness and misery I know you've been there:
    in Jesus, you've overcome everything that's evil.

8. In relating to other people,
    your kingdom comes alive for me:
    in love, I can feel that you are with us.

9. Some say you are not a family God:
    in order to know you fully, they say, I have to be alone;

10. yet Jesus knew the conflicts of home and family:
    and your Spirit is known in relationships with others.

11. How can I love you, unless I love my neighbours:
    your love is like that of my nearest and dearest.

12. In our difficulties, we learn to cry for your help:
    in our joys, we recognise your continued presence.

13. As sorrow approaches, we look to you for strength:
    in bereavement and loneliness, I find your firm support.

14. At the end I know that you are with me:
    as you were in my beginning, so be close to me forever.

A FRAMEWORK FOR TODAY?

Star Wars is about the great battle that takes place between the galaxies. It seems to have created quite a large following, a sort of "Dr Who" for another generation, superbly OK, with the right people winning in the end.

First, the mythological beings of space provide a new world. They may be obviously dressed up actors, but they provide a wonderful fantasy world, jumping into a space craft to travel through a few million light years with the sort of ease we normally jump into a car to drive a few miles.

Secondly it is about 'goodies' and 'baddies' but it is interesting that the good people hide at "the rebel headquarters". We aren't used to the good people being rebels! So the good robot is all in gold, while Darth Veda is dressed in black. He is the Lord of Darkness, a fallen angel, just as in the mythology of Satan.

Thirdly, there is a supernatural force to be reckoned with. The man engaged as a pilot doesn't believe in it, and anyway he is in business for the money he can earn. The believers are the young man and the old man, though the pilot comes round in the end, of course. Faith is more difficult for a middle-aged man of the world.

Fourthly, there is the art of learning to rely on the force. "May the force go with you!" It needs practising – when you think about what you're doing (wielding a laser sword, for example) you can't succeed, but when you're in tune with the force and stop thinking so hard about yourself, it all works. It is rather like the philosophy of Zen.

Star Wars provides a new mythology for faith. It is far more important religious material for us than Stars on Sunday. The four ideas might be just like the four things picked on by the Acts of the Apostles to epitomise the life of the early church:

> the apostles' teaching (may the force go with you), and fellowship (the rebels who are good guys), the breaking of bread (the liturgy of the space age stories) and the prayers (how you get in touch with the force).

Of course, we can all catch a glimpse of what that may be like from our own experience of working with other people. Much of the time we can be frustrated and the reality doesn't match our expectations. We know what it's like to be excited and expect great things, only to discover it's raining or dad's being rotten to me, or the magic doesn't seem to be working any more. My journey of faith doesn't lead to sitting comfortably in a deck chair in the sunshine! It is a journey from certainties into mystery. The same journey is being made more recently through the imagery of Harry Potter or the Lord of the Rings, perhaps.

The Clan of the Cave Bear is a novel about prehistoric man, or rather, woman. It's a story about a small girl losing all her family in an earthquake, but unable to survive by herself. She is picked up by a Neanderthal clan, who look after her. But she is not one of them; she is bigger, more intelligent, more like a modern human being. She is a stranger among the clan, different, lonely, misunderstood. Yet she has abilities and leadership qualities, strength and determination. She is also something of a threat to them! In other words, it's a novel about today and about us. The business of belonging is very complex. Sometimes we can only approach it by mythology, by seeing it played out in another kind of language and story from the one we are used to. That is at least in part the function of the religious journey, too.

PSALM

1. God, why is our life so complicated:
   why have you made other people so different from me?

2. Yet we have been seeking you for centuries:
   the religious quest has occupied each generation.

3. The variety of Hindu gods shows us your diversity:
   our lives surrounded by your two-eyed truth.

4. Meditations of Buddhists proclaim serenity:
   reverently monks remember their rules.

5. Jews keep Bible festivals in their homes:
   stressing the value of law and telling their stories.

6. Christians believe in your forgiveness:
   their faith rooted in history but open to your future.

7. Islam gives strength in the search for perfection:
   a single-minded pursuit of goodness in daily living.

8. Many religions have fostered human unity:
   the inspiration of Sikhs revealed in the Gurus.

9. Some of us are divided by common scriptures:
   cultures of east and west can keep us apart,

10. but we can also delight in our differences:
    breathe in us all your Spirit of peace.

11. Help us respect one another's moral struggles:
    give us your power to support each other's prayer -

12. widen the hearts of all of us to deepen our devotions:
    may you be for us our magnet and our wings.

KEEPING THE RULES

Once upon a time, I had to preach regularly to a largely wealthy congregation. On occasions, I felt I was expected to preach about the text where Jesus says that a camel going through the eye of a needle would be an easier operation than a rich person finding a way to the Kingdom of God. It didn't ever go down too well! We always seem to be in danger of seeming to believe that there has to be a new law (a bit like the Ten Commandments) that we expect Christian people to keep, there just are things you ought to be doing. If you don't keep this law, then you're not a proper Christian, and you will go to hell. And that, of course, is a heresy anyway, because each of us is loved by God. As St Paul kept on saying, you don't have to be a good keeper of law to be loved by God, you simply have to trust.

What might a new law be like anyway? As a child, I was expected to learn the Ten Commandments by heart. They say: no other god; no images (or idols); don't swear by God; keep the sabbath day – the four commandments about God; then the six commandments about other people – respect your parents, don't kill anyone, commit adultery, steal, accuse anyone falsely, nor want anything that belongs to someone else.

One alternative list might be the seven deadly sins, another list it is quite hard to remember: hatred, envy, greed, lack of care, lust, anxiety and pride. But this is another negative list, and so it is sometimes balanced by the list St Paul suggests to the people of Galatia: love, joy, peace (I can remember the first three quite easily!), patience, kindness, goodness, faithfulness, gentleness and self-control.

Dr David Jenkins once said that he thought our society had two sins. (Ah, that begins to sound a bit better.) To read the papers, watch the television or even listen to the radio, you might think those two would be sex and violence, though that is not what he meant. He was speaking about greed and sensuality. Sensuality is a bit more than sex and I suppose it could be said to include violence, too. I think it means treating people as objects instead of subjects, and being selfish about our own needs and desires. Greed is a bit more than just wanting to be a millionaire. Perhaps it means wanting more, however much we might or might not have, and usually at the expense of someone else. You might say that both of these two are simply modern forms of selfishness. That I can understand, and I might even be able to remember that law without too much difficulty.

But isn't all of this a bit negative? Shouldn't we be looking for something positive again? So we tend to remember the two halves of the Ten Commandments in their positive form, about loving God and loving our neighbour. For, of course, any new law is not just a matter of having to do as you're told. It's rather more important than that. Yet we live in a society that loves a bit of confrontation. We like to see the two sides slug it out, as in a film, or at Wimbledon or Cardiff, where there can be a winner and a loser. We want to blame someone who is wrong, and occasionally praise someone who is right. It's much the same at home. Can you have rules any more about the time for young people to be home (for example), so that everything is cut-and-dried or black-and-white? What do you do when there's a row? What if your daughter wants to marry a Muslim, or your son to shack up with someone you don't approve of? Parents – and children – often seem trapped, unable to do anything, and forgiveness is not easy. As a society, we cannot cope with some crimes, especially against children.

It's like the angry parent, who tries the line about 'doing what you're told' and then throws at you the terrible follow-on command, 'and you'll like it!' A new law would be about caring so much that you want to do everything you can to please the other person. We are all of us really rather good at that – we're quite good at doing it for our cat or dog, we're pretty good (most of the time) at doing it for our parents or children; we're extremely good at doing it for our partner, husband or wife. And, in doing any of that, we are after all learning what it means to love God. As St Paul said, we are looking, not just for a new law, but for a new world – the old order has gone and a new order has already begun, when anyone is 'in Christ.'

Being conscious of the presence of God makes you a new person. To practice the presence of God is what Brother Lawrence suggested we might be trying to do, all the time.

PSALM

1. How can anyone live a moral life?:
    by following God's commandments.

2. Put your trust in God:
    for other things will prove to you
    how untrustworthy they are!

3. Give praise to God for a miracle:
    but don't demand another one when you want it.

4. Practise the presence of God:
    for God is with you always.

5. So, avoid the hatred that divides you
    from your neighbours:
    the envy that leads you to wanting what others have;

6. the greed which exploits the labour of human beings:
    and lays waste the good earth
    our descendants will need;

7. the indifference which ignores
    the plight of the homeless:
    the lust which uses the bodies of women and men;

8. the anxiety that looks for popularity:
    and the pride that leads you to trust only in yourself.

9. Love your neighbour as yourself:
    treat others, as you would wish to be treated.

PRAYING

"Lord, teach us to pray..."

It is perhaps a pity that, in the Luke Gospel, the answer to this lovely question is only a form of words, a prayer, together with the suggestion that we should be persistent in praying, so God will take note of our requests. The Matthew Gospel at least puts it in the context of other bits of teaching about praying. But it is easy to get the impression that praying is all about saying prayers, and especially praying for someone or some thing. Actually, that kind of praying is not as easy as it sounds, and many of us are not that good at it. Why do monks and nuns spend a lifetime learning to do it?

Praying is a job for life in another sense, too. Bill Vanstone, the brilliant vicar in Lancashire, used to say that some people were able to pray, other people were better at polishing the church floor till it shone. And the cleaners were praying just as much by what they did as the pray-ers by what they said. St Benedict is supposed to have coined the phrase that "working is praying." I remember learning the lesson from the Iona Community. We were expected to join in the prayers of the Community in the Abbey, but it was just as much expected that we join in the work of the Community. That was not just peeling the spuds for dinner, but also helping to rebuild the Abbey. So powerful was that lesson that there are occasions, just sometimes, when work becomes a bit hard for me, and the backache takes over, that I still think "laborare est orare" – working–is praying.

There are other ways of 'agonising' that are also praying. There was once a movement called "The Quiet Room" – in London there was such a place, and those who had arranged for it would say that they hoped it might become a place where people would go when they need to think what they had to do next. It is not a bad definition of praying. And suffering is praying, too. Of course, pain can be so overwhelming that you cannot be expected to make it into prayers, into forms of words to be spoken, because the suffering itself is the praying. Ultimately, probably the best shot any of us will ever make at praying properly may well be in dying. Cecily Saunders, the person largely responsible for the hospice movement, has another lovely phrase about dying; she says that, in the end, it means "letting go and letting God."

Naturally, actual words and prayers are important, too. Without using other people's words, I should never be able to find my own; without finding some of my own words, even if only very vaguely in my head, I should never begin the process of putting myself constantly in the presence of God. Without the awareness of God loving me, I should never have a notion of praying at all.

It was a churchwarden of about 50 or so who once told me that every night, before he went to sleep, he would say what he was taught at his mother's knee, "Gentle Jesus, meek and mild, look upon a little child." Part of me was shocked by the revelation that he had not grown any further than that. Alan Ecclestone used to say that praying came down to three very simple things. We all very easily find occasions to say "God, help me!" That is perhaps the most basic of all prayer. It is possible to go beyond that to the equally simple and profound prayer, "Thank God!" The third prayer is one that probably has no words, but is simply the act of letting go. (The Luke Gospel at the death of Jesus puts it in the simple words, "Father, into your hands I commend my spirit.")

PSALM

1.   I don't know how to pray:
     my God, you're far away from me.

2.   The words don't come easily any more:
     phrases I know by heart don't seem so genuine.

3.   My energy is drained, you don't feel near me:
     dryness and boredom have taken a hold on me;

4.   I know you're close but I cannot see you:
     you seem to be here, but out of focus.

5.   My life's full of tensions, I'm not able to relax:
     stresses and strains make me certain I cannot cope.

6.   God, you are nearer to me than my breathing:
     yet my heart goes blank and my mind won't grasp you.

7.   Others have travelled this road before:
     why do I have to struggle to find the way for myself?

8.   Be close to me again, let me feel your presence:
     help me hold my mind in my heart,

9.   give life to the dry bones of my will:
     bring renewal to my tired understanding,

10. then I'll thank you with all my power:
     and praise you from the depths of my being.

EIGHT

LIVING

EXPERIENCES OF LIFE

A significant part of our experience is connected with birth, marriage and dying, in whichever part of the year it happens!

Baptism has always been a problem in England. The first Roman Emperor to become a Christian was proclaimed Emperor at York, about 1800 years ago. And, ever since, it seems that many people in England have felt the same way that he did. He thought that baptism washed away your sins. But, afterwards of course, you might very easily get dirty again. So he decided he would not get baptised until he was on his deathbed. There is one story that, in the end, he died suddenly and was never baptised at all, and that probably would have upset him even more!

But there are people who jump in the other direction today. They feel that the baby must be done because then he'll get on well. There's a kind of magic to the ceremony; it will wash away the evil, or the devil. And that's the reason why, in the old days, it used to be the job of the godmother to pinch the baby's bottom, to make sure that there would be some crying. So long as the baby cried, then the devil would be let out!

Actually, baptism is none of those things. Baptism is really a sign, for us, a sign of God's love. In the same sort of way as the Communion is a sign of God's love for us. A small baby cannot possibly be that evil, yet, there hasn't been enough time for him to have done terribly bad things (except perhaps at 3 o'clock in the morning on the odd night?). The baby cannot possibly decide that she wants to become a Christian, and yet parents have brought her for baptism as a Christian, without asking her permission. And that is how God deals with all of us. God does not ask us first whether we have done anything bad, or whether we would like him to love us. He just does. He does not ask any of us whether we would like to be called to follow Jesus. He just calls. Then, it's up to us.

Every Step of the Way

So God loves a small baby in the same way as he loves us. We do not have to be perfect to earn God's love and we do not have to be about to die either. We just have to be prepared to respond. That's all!

WEDDING PSALM

1. The church bells greet the blushing bride:
   the bridegroom welcomes her to his side
   with a nervous smile.

2. In front of their families and friends they declare their love:
   they commit their lives to one another
   in the presence of God.

3. "All that I am I give to you:
   and all that I have I share with you."

4. Blessed are you, the God of our parents:
   you give joy to husband and wife.

5. Blessed are you, Lord Jesus Christ:
   you too were present at a wedding in Galilee.

6. Blessed are you, Holy Spirit of God:
   when we are together, you are between us.

7. As we know each other in love:
   may we feel your love more deeply, God of love;

8. when we let each other down:
   may we know that you will never forsake us.

9. For a wedding is another beginning again:
   the triumph and fulfilment of all our hopes.

10. We build our future on marriage and family life:
    we can have better marriages as we enrich our lives.

11. We celebrate the magic and the mystery of love:
    grant us to live through our failures
    and find greater glories.

THE STRUGGLE OF LIFE

So often, people are hurt. We find other people difficult, and they tell us off, so we feel inferior and "put down." We find marriage and home life difficult, and we get into a rut of not facing up to it, so we begin to feel angry, frustrated, unhappy, shouted at, not cared for. Or we feel lonely, since nobody understands what I feel, and everybody's too busy to care anything for me, so I don't have any real friends, and even in a crowd I feel alone. Or else, we are just hurt, in an accident, because of an illness or disease, and things are wrong with us.

We all know what it's like to feel hurt. Can religion help us, at all?

Well, of course it was a long time ago, but Jesus actually knows what it's like to feel hurt. That's what Christianity's all about. Christ is at the centre of faith. And he knows. What is more, because he is still around, it's irrelevant that it was so long ago, because he still knows about me. I don't know whether he is going to be able to wave a magic wand and make my hurt any better (he doesn't usually seem to work like that, actually) but he sure does know what it's like.

I wonder if you have ever had the experience of trying to deal with yourself, when you feel really badly hurt. I'm not just thinking of being ill. I mean being hurt by other people. The worst pain is probably the pain that is in your head, or rather in your heart. Pills won't do much to help that, only other people. And they don't always realise. Have you ever gone out of your way to really look for help from other people? Someone was telling me they had done that, expecting to find great help from their church, and about half of them were marvellous. But the other half were like anybody else, unhelpful, got the wrong end of the story, didn't understand, or made things worse. Well, maybe 50% is not a bad proportion. Most people don't help you.

Perhaps, nevertheless, you would expect every person in a church to be marvellous. Is the church not in the business of healing people? Oddly enough, it doesn't seem to be. It may be in the business of teaching people. It is in business to keep the worship of God going, and building an organisation to do that and other things needs money, so it needs to raise money too. There is a lot to do that is not remotely concerned with healing people. Often, when we are feeling hurt, we forget that. Only a few people are going to begin to understand.

Some churches do major on healing and say that the church should be doing what Jesus did. Even so, they are not too keen on promising miracle cures. People are often prepared to spend time with you, but not necessarily promising to cure your arthritis.

I have often been helped by a distinction between illness and disease. A disease is what the doctor reckons you have, or the bad situation you find yourself in. It can sometimes be cured, sometimes not. The doctor can explain how it might be done, although there are times when the medical expert can't hold out hope of a complete cure. You can't cure cancer, always. But more important than disease is the illness you feel inside. You don't want a "cure" for that: you can't cure a broken marriage, you can't often cure loneliness, and by definition you can't cure bereavement. But you can treat them in various ways, especially if you catch them early. You want healing. It takes time, and it needs other people.

Doctors don't always have time for that. Clergy are not always too good at it. Christian people do not always seem to think it important. Yet it is perhaps the most important thing you can do for anyone else, to heal them, to heal the hurt they feel. I have done it sometimes, I know, and I bet you have done it several times without even knowing. In fact, it may be better if you don't know. Because it is God who does the healing, not you or me. If I knew every time, I might get a bit big headed and think it was me! But healing of this kind happens every day, and you do not have to be an expert. You just have to care. Someone once produced a definition for this kind of love: "To make the concerns of the other person the most important for you." That's healing for you.

PSALM OF DESPAIR

1. It's raining outside, there's nothing I can do:
   a cloud of depression settles over my mind.

2. God, I am useless:
   what's the point of living
   when there's nothing but failure?

3. There's no joy in anything I do:
   a great heavy weight presses down on my shoulders.

4. I've no hope and no particular friends:
   they used to be my support
   and they've left me alone.

5. What have I done wrong:
   is there a special reason for you to punish me?

6. They'll put me back into hospital:
   but they can't see what's in my mind.

7. No one understands my feelings:
   all I can hope for is to sleep forever.

8. I'm afraid of other people:
     the only thing to do is tell no one and stay by myself.

9. Everyone's against me, they are persecuting me:
     it's because I've committed such crimes that
     they're trying to kill me.

10. Now I'm confused, so I call on you:
     I don't know what is happening;
     help me mother my despair.

11. If only I can trust in someone - don't fail me now:
     there must be some way out,
     and you can understand me.

BELIEVING IN LIFE

Once upon a time, I was "our man at St Mark's" Church, and was for that reason responsible for administering what was called "Gale's Charity." It provided the princely sum of £4 to be distributed to poor people by the Vicar and Churchwardens. For their trouble, they were themselves allowed to take from the charitable funds a sum of 50p to have a drink afterwards. Additionally, the vicar got a further 50p for preaching a sermon on the day of the distribution. That was to be St Thomas's day, December 21st. Can you imagine vast numbers of people stopping their pre-Christmas rush and diverting their energy into listening to a sermon, no matter what day of the week it happened to be?

Some time ago, all that changed, fortunately. The Charity Commissioners stopped worrying about whether the sermon was actually preached, and amalgamated the funds with others to make a more respectable charity that was able to give money in ways that helped local people today. And we stopped trying to remember Thomas just before Christmas, and keep his day in July. It has a great deal to do with India.

Thomas is mentioned in the lists of the 12 disciples of Jesus, but only the John Gospel has anything to say about him: "Thomas, called Didymus" – or, in more modern Bibles, "Thomas who was called the Twin." Didymus is the Greek word for a twin, and Thomas is a Hebrew word for a twin. There is just a chance that his name was really Judas Thomas, or Judas the twin. That is where the story comes from that he was the brother of Jesus (in the Mark Gospel 6.3) and so possibly even his twin brother. The John Gospel has three stories about him. When Lazarus was dead, he resigned himself to the obvious fate of Jesus (but also expressed his deep commitment to following him) by saying, "Let us go, so that we can die with him." Then he put into words the question all the disciples were thinking, when Jesus told them he was going to leave them – but we don't know where you're going, so how can we know the way? And thirdly, he took the prime place in the Easter story of the Upper Room. Jesus had appeared when Thomas wasn't there, so he said that he would never believe they had really seen Jesus risen from death, unless he could physically put his finger in the wounds in his hands and his fist into the huge gash in his side. For this he is often called "Doubting Thomas" as a result. But the odd thing is that, when it was the next Sunday, and they saw Jesus in the Upper Room again, when Thomas was there, he wasn't a doubter at all. On that occasion, he produced the greatest act of belief in the risen Christ in the whole of the Gospels, calling him "my Lord and my God." He would better be called "believing Thomas" instead.

Perhaps doubt and belief are closer together than we think. The opposite of belief is not doubt; you need to have doubts and questions in order to believe anything that is really important. The opposite of belief is more like despair. Once again, as Bishop John Robinson pointed out, the John Gospel has come up with a story that seems somehow more authentic and more original (going back behind the other Gospels) as if it had been written not last, but first of all.

Much later on, according to the tradition, it was Thomas who became the missionary to India. Recently, the tradition has had a bit more study, and seems surprisingly feasible. There was a regular trade route between Palestine and the western coast of the Indian sub-continent, apparently. It is not at all stupid to think of such a journey taking place in the first century (though it would have been more difficult later on). In India, Thomas was martyred, and buried near the city of Madras. The Syrian Orthodox Church was strong in India and has kept the faith handed down directly from the great apostle of faith. That "Mar Thoma" Church is one of the few eastern churches that has also been in full communion with the Church of England, since 1974, though retaining its Orthodox worship. It is that tradition that keeps his festival on July 3rd, rather than on the shortest and darkest day of the year. For Thomas is a sign of light and faith, including the necessary questions.

PSALM OF HOPE

1. Help me, God, to look ahead more hopefully:
   nothing like a death sentence to concentrate my mind.

2. I'm told I ought to plan for years ahead:
   but to settle for the next six months
   could be more creative.

3. If I could fix my sights on the immediate future:
   then I might get priorities in order.

4. The future can be deadly and uninviting:
   it's easy to postpone the important thing for a rainy day.

5. But this life's not a rehearsal:
   it's the only performance I've got;

6. help me now to be:
   what I'd like some day to become,

7. for faith's about this life not another one:
   religion not only for the next world, but for this!

8. Come, Holy Spirit, fill this moment:
   grant me, God, to be really myself,

9. to know today is always my meeting with you:
   to live this day as if it were my last.

ADVICE FROM EXPERIENCE

Ecclesiastes, the name of a book in the Bible, is an odd word. It makes you think of church, perhaps. But it means something more like "Mr Speaker" really. Or perhaps "the Leader of the House." It means a person who speaks in an assembly, the preacher, a person who speaks where many people will hear. People have sometimes wondered how this particular bit of Wisdom literature, or poetry, ever got into the Bible in the first place! It was once attributed to King Solomon, who was the person who had been everywhere and done everything, and was thought to be reflecting on his long life and what he had learned from it all.

Now, I'm not sure about other people, but the old man trying to give advice to the young never seems to me to be very successful. "Remember your Creator, in the days of your youth" has a certain poetic ring about it, but it didn't exactly persuade me to think about God when I was young. But the reflections of older people can certainly be extremely interesting, when they are not intended to "preach" at me, but to pass on their wisdom. And the advice in this book of the Bible seems very traditional and unexceptional.

Work hard, keep to the rules, make use of every opportunity (for you may not get another chance) and God will help you. It is the sort of advice the older generation in Britain may well try to give to the young. (But they would be bored by it, no doubt!)

Perhaps that is what Ecclesiastes, the Speaker, means by 'vanity of vanities' or 'futility' then? What is life all about? What are we here for? Is it simply a matter of going round and round in circles, achieving nothing? For the Hebrew view of life was that it moves in a straight line, with purpose and direction, following the guidance of God, rather than everything happening in cycles which keep on coming back again to the same point. Life is about being, as we say, "driven" to work at what you are committed to. Is the meaning of life simply a matter of getting all you can for yourself and walking over others to achieve it? Or is it more about being aware of your responsibilities (for God will bring us all under judgement, as the book says)?

This is, therefore, not just (maybe not at all) a reflection for young people! Older people are just as much in need of that kind of advice.

FUNERAL PSALM

1. I wasn't even able to say goodbye:
    why have you removed him away from me
    so suddenly?

2. Why should this happen to me:
    he had done nothing to deserve such treatment.

3. They said to me, "Do not weep":
    am I not to cry for the loss of my companion;

4. even the greatest have wept in disappointment:
    am I not also allowed to express my feelings?

5. They said, "Keep busy", but already I'm exhausted:
    they said, "Time will heal", but still it hasn't done so.

6. Help me to manage my memories:
    whatever I recall brings only pain and grief.

7. Yet I find comfort in my friends:
    in their presence is a token of your care;

8. their loving embrace is a sign of your support:
    the kindness of a handshake
    can speak of your graciousness.

9. In your presence, I can face what has happened:
    grant me to accept it, as you accept me.

10. The past is not fixed for ever:
    help me reap more treasures from all my experience,

11. nor is the past something lost for eternity:
    my friendship and my joy are not gone for ever;

12. for as I remember, I glimpse what you see always:
    now you see him face to face, as you see me.

13. Continue to be with me as I look ahead:
    give me courage to rebuild my life for your future.

EVERY STEP OF THE WAY

NINE

FESTIVALS

WE'RE ALL IN THIS TOGETHER

Once upon a time, there was a big house on the hill that was home for severely mentally handicapped girls and women. At "The Mount" was a young woman called Lucy who found life very difficult, but somehow felt that she had to go fighting on, in spite of problems that seemed like a mountain all around her. One day she opened the local paper and read the headline, "Mount to be closed." The bottom dropped out of her world. She thought she would be put out on the street. She thought of committing suicide. Her struggle was obviously too much for her. Yet she found that there were people who seemed to be working for her – lots of people came to the Mount, someone started getting signatures on a petition. There were meetings and protests with local Councillors and Members of Parliament. It was all a bit confusing. Somehow it just seemed that the fight was going to continue and Lucy would, after all, have to go on struggling.

Once upon another time, a young man called Mark went to Ulster to work in what's called "community development." He was a bit left wing, but determined to give everything he could to work with young people and bring some help to the bitter communities of Northern Ireland. His mate, he found, was a very different sort of a person, a pacifist. One day this friend was killed in an explosion caused by a terrorist bomb, and his wife and her family were very badly hurt, too. Mark was shattered. But soon, he realised this was what his work was all about. He decided to continue his work with even greater determination, now he knew what people felt like. He would try to make sure he didn't fall into the trap of hatred or retaliation, but go on struggling.

Once upon yet another time, high and mighty people gathered at a Church Conference in Africa and one of the delegates was Karen from the UK. It was an amazing experience with people from every continent. She began to see what incredible strides the churches have already made towards unity, and she took part in the very moving worship and ceremonies of a great international gathering. But she couldn't help thinking of the church at home, and how far we still have to go to learn anything about real local unity. After all, it all began back in 1910 in

Edinburgh, and she was hearing about the great strides that had been made in India since 1934 and how, in some places a handful of conservative churches had made the whole thing quite impossible. She met people whose hopes had been crushed, yet they had gone on working hard. Rome was not built in a day, and of course it all takes time. Much had been done, but much remained to do. She would go home and tell them that.

Once upon a time... Stories we can all multiply may seem depressing. But we know that the world can be a struggle. We ought to. Listening to the stories of the Gospel, we may think those kind of exploits are not for us; our life is supposed to be easy. When suffering comes our way (I mean the kind that turns our world upside down), we are inclined to say, "Why should this happen to me?" Jesus knew differently, and said he had to suffer. Perhaps you know the text that someone put in the Anglia Water Authority's headquarters at the time of the great drought years in the 1970s. They began to think then that the climate was changing and all their previous ideas would have to be revised.

> "Out of the gloom, a voice said to me
> 'Smile and be happy: things could be worse'
> So I smiled and was happy.
> And, behold, things did get worse."

A religious hope does not mean that difficulties are removed. In a sense it really does mean that things get worse! As the famous prayer says, "It is not the beginning of a thing that yieldeth the true glory, but the continuing of the task until it be thoroughly finished." Endurance is not always popular, but it is our business. We know a bit about how hard is the struggle, and how much we need to keep a vision of God and his Kingdom in front of us. In the middle of threats of exile, or worse, prophets and leaders in the Bible can write marvellous hymns of praise to God.

Being human means engaging in a journey that inevitably means some difficulty and struggle. Like Frodo Baggins of Bag End! Some people feel that Lord of the Rings reflects the gathering gloom of World War 2, but J R R Tolkein said it was not in his mind at the time. Frodo had to destroy the magic ring, and the only way to do it involved a hard and perilous journey. Or like the broadcast made by King George VI before he died, in which he quoted the American poem, "I said to the man who stood at the gate of the year, 'Where shall I go?' And he said, 'Put your hand into the hand of God. That shall be for you better than any known way.'"

PSALM

1. To start on a journey is difficult enough:
      but by coming together at first
      we can make a beginning.

2. Keeping together in our search is progress:
      real success will appear in our working together.

3. How pleasant it is to be together:
      the starting of a partnership is always a honeymoon!

4. But then how awful that other one becomes:
      why are the others so selfish when we are together?

5. If that's how it seems to them, then what of me:
      how difficult a person am I for the others to cope with?

6. For I'd never noticed what failings I have:
      but when we are working together
      it's hard to avoid them!

7. At last I realise how good our God is:
      how patient you are with us all
      and with our impossibilities.

TRANSFIGURATION

There is a gap in the diagram of the year's festivals, and it could be filled with the Transfiguration, coming within the Sundays after Trinity. Ethelbert Stauffer in the 1950s produced a timetable for the life and ministry of Jesus and dates this event in September 31 CE, which could well be at the autumn equinox (Jesus and His Story: SCM Press: 1960). The Luke Gospel story clearly puts it at sunset (Luke 9. 28-36).

"There's glory for you," said Humpty Dumpty and what he meant was "there's a nice knock-down argument for you." "But 'glory' doesn't mean 'a nice knock-down argument' "Alice objected."When I use a word," Humpty Dumpty said in rather a scornful tone, "it means just what I choose it to mean."

Every Step of the Way

Charles Dodgson was presumably not writing Alice Through the Looking Glass about the festival of the Transfiguration. But he produced a nice knock-down text for it! For the festival of Jesus standing at the top of a holy mountain and being changed in appearance and seen with the religious representatives of the Law and the Prophets, Moses and Elijah, is certainly about glory. And it certainly is not a knock-down argument, in the sense of being about an 'event' that makes everything crystal clear to anybody who happens to be passing at the time. In the story, it was not even clear to the disciples who participated in it, and who were so puzzled they did not know what they were saying. It was the time of the Feast of Tabernacles, harvest time, so they blurted out something about building tents for the religious figures they saw before them, overawed by their presence.

There was a certain logic about keeping the festival of the Transfiguration on mid-Lent Sunday, because the story so clearly looks forward to the suffering and death of Jesus. It is a kind of mid-way story of the disciples' understanding of him, too. The Gospel story of Jesus has moved from a ministry of healing and popularity, to the forward movement to passion and death, "setting his face" to go to Jerusalem. Keeping it in August often has meant it comes at holiday time, and been an ignored part of the tradition. It is a strange story about glory. One definition of what 'glory' really does mean is that it is about seeing something ordinary and finding yourself looking at God. It may be just the sunset, but we may call it 'glorious' because it takes on for us a quality of something much more than just a dying sun and a few clouds. Or we say that a sportsman or public figure has achieved glory by finding just the right time to score a goal, or just the right phrases to encapsulate our feelings.

"There's more in this than meets the eye" is a phrase we sometimes use to express the transfigurations we experience, when ordinary things seem to take on greater significance for us. "This thing is bigger than both of us" is the feeling lovers sometimes try to express to one another. We all know the experience of being in the presence of something that puzzles us and yet brings glory. But just as the experience of God is something that happens to most of us occasionally (not frequently), so the consciousness of glory is something we are not necessarily aware of every day. The trick is to remember, even to prolong the awareness and to allow ourselves to live on the strength of it. For the story comes at a time when Jesus was praying for strength to go forward, as the Gospel puts it, "the dying that Jesus would achieve in Jerusalem." Transfiguration for us is also about change and transformation, seeing things we had not expected, or seeing people in a new light, or recognising how we too are going to have to face up to a future we had not taken on board.

In just that way, several people have told me, many of us have never really taken on board the existence of the 21st century. It was so far in the future, when we were children; it was after we were due to retire; or it was a time when I should be so very old that clearly I should have died by then! And yet, here we are, well into the new century. That's a simplistic image of transfiguration, but it helps me understand it a little more.

PSALM

1. As I bend to light the fire in my hearth:
   Holy Spirit, I kneel to lay my life before you.

2. Kindle a flame in my heart today:
   light your love in me so it will last forever.

3. For your love can warm me and those I love:
   your inspiration fires my neighbours and my friends.

4. You brighten the way for all my family:
   bring new light for us and our community.

5. Fulfil my heart's desire to be taken up in you:
   let me continue to guard the holy fire.

6. Then your glory will burn forever within us:
   warming the world with prayer and fervent praise.

HAPPINESS

If you call someone a "bloody" fool, I was always told, you are not accusing them of having cut their finger, but you are swearing "by Our Lady." Nowadays, when we use the word "blessed" we don't often think we are referring to the Mother of Jesus, either. "Blessed kids!" we say. Blessed seems a bit remote, as a title of beatification, and it sounds odd when it is applied to someone recently dead and not yet a saint.

And then Mary is the Virgin, too. Whatever your views about the stories, technically the "parthenogenesis" or virginal conception, it still seems strange as a title. We respond more to the cartoon about the wise and foolish virgins, when the latter were locked out from the wedding because they were not ready, but one looked to another of the foolish ones and said, "Well, at least we are virgins!" Perhaps we should be calling Mary a mother, rather than ever virgin? It sounds as if we are still wanting to say that virginal is the best possible state to be. Apart from being counter-cultural today, it is not being single that is preferred (for she was married), the problem appears to be sex!

So it is good to think of St Mary's Church or St Mary's Day, rather than anything blessed or virginal. Even Great St Mary's or Santa Maria Maggiore is better than that.

On the other hand, Mary is important as a woman in heaven. Some say she provides the feminine element in God, as she is Queen of Heaven, the senior of all the saints. We try sometimes to squeeze a female role for God, and speak of God our father and mother. Some see Sophia (wisdom) as a female form of God. No doubt the discussions will continue. At least Mary is female, all right.

And blessed can mean happy, as well as beatified. Again, it has not been especially popular in religious terms to be "happy." For some Christians, to be happy might almost be a sign of being sinful, since religion has to be about suffering and pain. Yet we are wrong to forget that, even on the Cross, according to the John Gospel, Jesus was caring for his mother and ended his life with a cry of triumph, "I've done it!" (It is accomplished). Our world does seem to be fond of asserting our right to enjoyment, fulfilment, achievement and happiness. Perhaps, as we get older, these things become more important, rather than less. And there is another title of Mary, which we do not use all that often, but which says the same thing. Just after World War 1 it was official. Mary is the "Mediator of all Graces." She is a person who helps us find real happiness.

PSALM

1.   Let your children come to you, our God:
     like a hen collects her brood, to keep them safe;

2.   as Jesus wept over his people:
     you cry over us, our pride and our failings.

3.   But you, our God, are our mother
     and treat us with gentleness:
     you gather us together, like children, for protection;

4.   you comfort us in sorrow and nurse us in sickness:
     with the milk of heaven you feed us
     and soothe away our pain;

5.   tenderly you show us your care:
     you shield us from hatred and fear;

6. you draw us to your side for warmth and company:
   holding our hand you give us comfort and strength.

7. Despair turns to hope through your loving embrace:
   and with your gracious encouragement
   we find ways to grow up.

8. In your mercy and compassion, re-make us:
   we are born to new life by your love.

THE JOY OF GIVING

My wife was a Methodist (as well as an Anglican, as it happens, and that might be a lesson for us all), so I perhaps absorbed a thought that is perhaps especially Methodist. It is an amused questioning about the way, in many churches, we take the collection. It is usually during the hymn after the sermon has been preached. That means it gives the impression that we will pay according to how good we think the preacher is. Actually, of course, that is not what "the offertory" is for at all! We come to church to hear God speak to us again; we respond to that Word by giving ourselves, or maybe just a very small token of ourselves, as an offering. That may seem very obvious. I have a suspicion it is not always at the top of our consciousness. Giving is my response to what God had given me.

Various groups make little rules about it, to make life easier for us. There's the tradition of "tithing" which is the giving of 10% of my income. Many people will include in the tenth, what they give to charitable causes of different kinds, not just a church. The Iona Community requires its members to take part in Economic Discipline. One way of doing that is to work out $2\frac{1}{2}$ % of my disposable income, and to make that my donation to the Community Fund. Wonderfully Scottish, but at least an attempt to be as fair as possible to a wide range of individuals and families. Christian Giving, we are often told, is not about putting a bit of my spare cash on the plate, but about ensuring that I give to God, before I spend on other things. So the rule is a simple, if profound, one: God first, other people next, and myself last.

In any case, giving is going to mean budgeting. I have sometimes been struck by how some families seem to get by without any sort of budgeting at all. I was never taught how to do it; it was forced on me. Perhaps others have the same experience. And yet it is basic to any kind of Christian stewardship of my resources. I need to know what my resources are, before I can make any kind of contribution. Mr Micawber's advice still stands: "Income 20 shillings Expenditure 20 shillings and 6 pence Result misery; Income 20 shillings Expenditure 19 shillings and 6 pence Result happiness."

That may sound as if Christianity has to be regimented and organised, and may feel a bit too much like being in the office again. There must still, I think, be room for giving that is spontaneous, so there should be some sort of leeway in our budget for giving, too. But there are also times when it is not sensible, and not Christian, to be giving money just because someone is asking you for it. Sympathy is a fine thing; we also need to exert our own judgement.

PSALM

1. Father in heaven we come to meet you:
   again as Jesus taught us
   we use your name and address!

2. Yet it's not in heaven but in this world where we meet you:
   our daily life and humanity
   are the world of your creation.

3. You've made us responsible for our world:
   you gave us what we have and what we are,

4. we are but stewards of your bounty:
   all good things are ours, held in trust from you.

5. Our money and our possessions are not ours by right:
   our time and our talents have been given us
   of your goodness,

6. we have to learn to be responsible stewards:
   to hold this earth in trust for our descendants,

7. to sit loose to what we say we own:
   throughout our earthly pilgrimage to travel light;

8. you've taught us what you require of your stewards:
   it's not what we do or fail to do,
   but our obedience you will judge.

9. Help us to value not success but faithfulness:
   grant us to see the real value of the money we use;

10. we can use worldly wealth to win ourselves some friends:
    not money, but the love of money, is the root of all evil.

11. It's not great wealth that we worship:
    we honour your faith in us that never wavers.

WORK

I persuaded my wife to go and choose a present in a shop. The assistant was very nice, realised we had come from a distance away, and asked, "Are you visiting?" "No," we said, "we are moving here soon." When she gave us the package, later, she said to us, "I hope you will enjoy living here." Some time later, I met the manager of that shop, and told him the story. He smiled, "All part of the training," he said. Well, of course it is.

It made me realise that God is like a shop manager. He wants his staff to be very friendly; they will be good to customers, and the customers will be happy and spend lots of money and advise others to do the same. It's always better when people are pleasant to you. Who wants the hassle, anyway? Naturally, people tend to be more pleasant when you are nice to them. So the best way to have happy people about is to be pleasant yourself. In the same way, when I was a curate, I was told to obey the words of the Psalm (in the old Coverdale version) to "grin like a dog and run about through the city." If God wants a good world, then he must train his staff to be pleasant and happy, because that will help make the world a better place. Like any good shop manager, he can't force staff to be happy, he has to trust us and help us by being pleasant himself and helpful so far as he can be. He will allow us to be miserable, when we feel that way, but hope that by showing us an example of being pleasant, we shall be good to other people, too. Simple, isn't it?

Well, no, it isn't simple at all! There are more important things than being pleasant. Like making money for the firm, or avoiding being walked over by competitors or bad customers. Jesus said as much. The children of this world are wiser than the children of light, and riches won't get you to heaven but you can use them to make friends. Of course, it is not easy. Whoever said it would be? Working in the service industry means being trodden on, not having any status, having a low paid job, and smiling when you are being shouted at. Now we do not live in an "upstairs, downstairs" world we have forgotten what it is like to be "in service." Interestingly, the society of Jesus' time knew about the treatment of slaves, and he said he was to be like a slave! God is the shop manager, and you can tell he looks happy all the time (even though he can't be – he is only human, after all!). And Jesus allows himself to be walked over by the customers, yet he still seems to come up smiling. So perhaps I have to try to be like that, too?

There was a day when someone introduced me to her daughter. "Isn't she a nice girl?" she said. I wasn't so sure. The daughter gave me a hard look and said, "What do you, as a chaplain, actually do?" Her mother didn't wait for me to reply, she said, "You know those days when I come home and I don't shout at

you? Well, those are the days when I've been able to shout at the chaplain instead."
I began to feel quite an important person, that day. Being pleasant is perhaps more important than we sometimes think, being walked over, maybe, when our feelings are not being respected, but when we can still be good towards others. Then we may be able to support and affirm them, just as God does to us all the time.

A friend once said to me, "God calls us to live in and affirm this moment, this place, this person, this experience." That's certainly true of the shop assistant; it's true of the industrial chaplain; it's true of the Christian. It is also true of Jesus, and so it is true of God.

PSALM

1. I enjoy my work, for you've given it to me:
    you are a God who works,
    and I work with your blessing.

2. You are there when I go to work in the morning:
    I meet you in my friends as we greet one another;

3. as we prepare for the day,
    you speak to us through others:
    you are in new ideas and the training we share;

4. my concentration reflects your loving care:
    your creative power inspires my thoughts
    and actions.

5. When I help another it's you that I meet:
    as I serve a customer, I am serving you;

6. when I am called to give account to my superiors:
    it's your judgement I face and you will judge in fairness.

7. If others treat me harshly, I am only your servant:
    Jesus was also the servant of others;

8. his work was to make your love visible:
    in my successes I, too, am completing
    your work of creation.

9. Long ago monks were taught that to work is to pray:
    help me see my task today as part of your purpose.

10. My achievements I offer to you:
    exhausted I give you my life.

(Published in Crucible and in CIPL Newsletter 1997)

HARVEST

Barry Lopez is a scientist who spent years travelling in the Arctic and studying its life. Yet he approached it with a kind of religious and poetic reverence. The Arctic is, of course, very different from our world. It is cold and dark. Of about 3,200 species of mammal we might find in the world, only 23 live north of the tree-line in the cold; of the 8,600 or so species of birds only 6 or 7 stay through the winter in the Arctic; out of about 30,000 species of fish, less than 50 have managed to live in the far north. Any animal, including human ones, which manages to live in such an inhospitable place deserves some special kind of praise. He describes the horned lark sitting on a nest on the ground with her three eggs, and no bigger than his fist. He looked down. She stared back, resolute as iron. So, Barry Lopez says, he took to bowing as he went on his walks, bowing with his hands in his pockets, towards the birds and the evidence of life in their nests, because of the life so unexpected and so hard to sustain.

To bow or genuflect to our world, the world of God's creation. That is what we do at Harvest. For God "saw what he had made, and it was good." Of course, it is fashionable to say that. We are all "green" these days. For we are in the new age, the Age of Mother Earth, when we are all more conscious of our place, that we come from earth and to the earth we shall return. We are just leaving the old age, the age of human creativity, the days of technology and science and industry. That was the age in which we found it hard to have faith in anything beyond ourselves, because we saw ourselves as the centre of the universe. But the new age is an age of greater belief, even if we still have science and technology, too. There are those who say this is a Bad Thing, a return to paganism and the past. But you cannot help noticing some interesting things, about God the creator, and the earth our mother. It is a bit like a harvest thanksgiving. A mixture of world government, peace, feminism, and a sort of Baha'i faith in the unity of God and the harmony of humanity.

A previous generation could be scathing. Harvest is the national festival of Saint Pumpkin! And loyal (myopic?) church people could be disparaging about those who came to church at harvest-time, as John Betjeman, with a wry smile, put in the mouth of the church mouse:

> But yet it's always strange to me,
> How very full the church can be,
> With people I don't see at all
> Except at Harvest Festival.

Every Step of the Way

Yet it is surprising how many people do celebrate harvest, around the world: North American Thanksgiving Days, the Jewish Feast of Tabernacles, and the half-term break (which used to be called "Potato-picking Week."). Harvest is a new festival, dating from 1862. Before that, there was a harvest home in the village hall, but nothing religious. The religious festival was Lammas Day (August 1st) to give thanks for the first loaf of bread, answering the prayers of Rogation (6th week of Easter) for blessing on the crops that had been sown. Celebrating the harvest when "All is safely gathered in" is quite modern. In an urban society, the fruits of the earth have been interpreted quite widely. I used to live in a seaside town, where the church was draped with fishing nets and lobster pots; in Sheffield, many churches used to be full of engineering and steel products; in some places you will find computers and electronic gadgets. So you do not have to be a farmer, or a craftsman or a flower arranger to want to celebrate harvest. It may be something that goes deeper into our subconscious memory, to express the inexpressible, to recognise that we belong to the world and that we are alive. Heaven help us if churches exist only for church celebrations!

A friend of mine in the country had invited us for a meal. "Now," somebody said, "shall we teach them the farmer's Grace? ... Hip, hip!" Everyone shouted "Hooray!" and dug into their food.

PSALM

1. My ancestor was our father Abraham
    who left his home and family:
    Israel a homeless refugee who settled in a foreign land.

2. There they became slaves and cried to God:
    they were treated badly but you saw their misery.

3. When they went they were few,
    but you made them a powerful nation:
    in your love you gave them a rich and fertile country,

4. so they brought you the first fruits from their land:
    tokens of harvest they offered to you.

5. Centuries later it's the same, we bring you our work:
    we still need a harvest thanksgiving
    to bring you the fruits of our toil,

6. though I can't live off my garden:
    my allotment won't make me a farmer
    like my forebears.

7. I live in an urban society:
   the symbols of harvest belong to the country;

8. others work for my food, I no longer live close to the earth:
   my health and welfare depend on people I do not know.

9. Nevertheless, my God, I bring you my life:
   bless the toil of my hands and my brain;

10. you have brought me also to an abundant heritage:
    I offer you a token of the harvest I share in every day.

(Published in Psalms for the Synod and TTTV)

Every Step of the Way

EVERY STEP OF THE WAY

TEN

THE KINGDOM SEASON

THE FUTURE

A feeling of loss and the awareness of self-confidence are two sides of the same coin. That seems appropriate for the autumn of the year, and the ending of the journey of the year of faith. After the long season of the Sundays after Trinity, there are four weeks of preparation for the beginning again of the year at Advent.

My son-in-law has a 12-year-old dog with arthritis, and they have been making the odd visit to the vet. One of the questions that arises in our minds, if not our conversation, at such times, is whether the dog has a future. For it is up to us to decide matters of life and death for our pets. We decide if the dog has a future. An idea that is completely foreign to the dog.

Maybe that is what makes us human, that we do have an idea of our future. Brian Keenan's moving story of his life as a hostage in Beirut, like other stories of prison, is remarkable for its belief in the future. There are attempts to escape, dreams about getting away and what I shall do when I am out of this dump. Even when treated like dogs, or in some cases far worse than dogs, human beings do still believe in a future.

Have we stopped doing that, or lost our confidence? Our institutions seem sometimes to be crumbling around us, just like the Berlin Wall. Terrorists threaten to destroy more than just walls. Are we able to believe in the future, any more? It is sometimes said that this is the first generation of parents to know that their children will not do better than they did. We take bread and wine, symbols of the earth. But has the earth a future? Perhaps we have already polluted it so badly that, like the dodos, we shall all come to a sticky end.

When things are bad, when faith is difficult, we take bread and wine, and we say they are the body and blood of Christ. There is some faith in that! When things are bad, when faith is difficult, we follow those with faith, even if we don't exactly know where we are going to. There is some faith in that! When things are bad, when faith is difficult, we wait on God and look for inner strength, and we say we believe in God and in ourselves. There is some faith in that! Faith in God, the father of our Lord Jesus Christ, and in God's Spirit within us.

Geoffrey Studdert Kennedy was a chaplain in World War 1, so he knew a thing or two about losing confidence in the future. One of his poems is called "Tragedy."

If life were only tragedy all through,
And I could play some high heroic part,
With fate and evil furies to pursue,
I would with steadfast heart,
But my fine tragic parts are never true.

God always laughs and spoils them, and for me
He sets the stage to suit a human fool,
Who blunders in where angels fear to be,
So if life is His School,
I trow He means to teach Humility.

PSALM OF THE HOSPICE

1.   What's happening to me, God, with this onset of pain:
        why are you bringing more suffering on me?

2.   It can't be true that you've let me down:
        nor fair for you to want to punish me -

3.   in me there's something that's no part of me:
        eating me up while I cannot control it.

4.   Will someone explain and say what's going on:
        talk to me, help me to know what is happening?

5.   Is this the end? Where can I get help:
        does anyone care that it's all so horrible?

6.   God, let me weep with you by day:
        sustain me with tears through the hours of the night.

7.   I need life packed up and ready to go:
        give me energy and time to work through the past.

8.   From those I have wronged I need forgiveness:
        those I love best can give me support.

116

9.   I'd like not to die insignificantly:
         but how can I manage my own destiny?

10. Still there's the pain, although it's controlled:
         I need your strength for the struggle ahead.

11. Help me be able to accept my self:
         then I'll be at peace with you and with others.

12. Just a few more people I need for a while:
         one relative's enough before I'm alone.

13. Let there be someone beside me now:
         I cannot speak but I can hear and understand.

14. Now at the last all is done:
         it is late, and I am ready.

15. So long as you are with me, that is all:
         now I can let go and let God.

16. Into your hands I commend my life:
         for you will redeem me and be merciful.

THE KINGDOM OF HEAVEN

The Kingdom of Heaven is like people running the Marathon.

Some of the runners are professionals, who set out to win, and (as St Paul said) only one of them will. This is a very small and "elite" group of runners, because this type of running is not for all of us, by any means, in spite of what St Paul said!

There are other runners whose aim will be to complete the race in a certain time, perhaps to do better than they have ever done before. They will not be expecting to win the race, and they will not be disappointed if they don't. They run, if anything, against themselves, the elements and the race, not competing against other people. They are out to complete the race in a "good time" for themselves, and it is all about believing in themselves.

But there is also a third group of runners who are there simply to do it. They do not expect to win, and the time they take is entirely irrelevant. All they are trying to do is to complete the course. Perhaps this is the majority of those who take part in a marathon race.

There are those three kinds of people in our world, too. Only few of us are here to succeed, against the opposition, to gain fame or fortune or whatever success means for us, to end up among the elite. A much larger group of us are here to race, if you like, against ourselves, so that our successes will be private ones, when we manage to do the best we can. In the world, there is also another group, and it is by far the largest group of all. These are the people whose main aim in life is just to survive. This may not be a large group in the western world, though there are a very large number, but in the Third World they will form the majority.

You do not have to win the race to belong to the Kingdom, either; you only have to survive.

PSALM

1. I would like to see you, Lord, in all your glory:
    I want to hear what you are saying in my world.

2. Why do I find it so hard to know you clearly:
    why's your activity shrouded in mystery?

3. The strike was nearly over and people were beaten:
    then there was the inkling of a new initiative,

4. but hope was soon dashed to pieces and gone:
    reconciliation denied,
    and everything looked like failure.

5. That day seemed to bring no light:
    yet the chance of redemption shone out like a beacon.

6. So you let us have just a glimpse of your presence:
    the sign of your Kingdom is an elusive vision.

7. For you do not dominate us with your power:
    your strength is seen most clearly
    in your being vulnerable.

8. I saw children in Soweto framed between the tanks:
    the young with their fists in salute,
    but their faces were grinning!

9. Their world seemed to have no hope:
    yet their hopefulness shone clear for all to see!

10. So you give us a sign of your presence:
    the glimpse of your Kingdom is a powerful vision.

ALL SAINTS

Laurie Lee wrote "Cider with Rosie" and it was published on condition that he wrote the blurb for it himself. Tongue in cheek he wrote that it was "destined to become a classic," and it did. So much so that, in his lifetime, it was on the syllabus for schools. Two girls, studying the book, arrived in Gloucestershire and found him sitting outside the pub. "Excuse me, sir," said one of them, "can you tell us where Laurie Lee is buried?"

I suppose we always assume that our heroes are dead, like the Princess Dianas and Mother Teresas as well as the saints of long ago, like the Venerable Bede or Saint Francis. They are known collectively as the Church Triumphant.

We do, in addition, sometimes take inspiration and encouragement from the saints we have known, who are not those that many other people would know about. I remember Norah, who had been brought up with the Plymouth Brethren but was moved to a new estate where the nearest church happened to be Church of England (and rather modern, too), so she attended it. She never agreed to be confirmed, to become an Anglican, because she felt that would have been to deny her early experience. But many of us regarded her as an honorary Anglican, and a friend of mine once said, "Don't worry about Norah; she is in the Kingdom already!" Such people are separated from saints, and we keep a day for All Souls to remember them; they are collectively the Church Expectant (those who wait).

But we do not often think of ourselves as saints. Yet we are also the Church Militant! (That is, for me, a bad phrase, implying that living is not really very important, only a struggle or a fight which we have to endure until we get to the real business of life when we have died). We are "called to be saints," as St Paul put it, and "fellow citizens with the saints, and part of the household of God." We are aware that we are happy, lucky ("blessed" as the Gospels say) to be among those who are called, but we try not to fall into the trap of saying, "I used to be cocky, but now I am perfect!"

But it is not the festival of the saints that most people celebrate; it is the night before. Halloween is really All Hallows Even, the night before the festival of All (hallowed) Saints. I suppose the idea began with a suspicion that, on the night before the festival, you could expect to see the witches and the ghosts of all the dead in the graveyard rise up to join in the festivities for their special day! Perhaps there is an unhealthy side of us that wishes always to be tied into the past, because the present is so hard to handle. It has sometimes seemed as if we were taught that the values of the past were much more important for us to keep, because the present has no values that are of any worth. It is always much easier to complain about how things have been going down hill since our (grand) parents' days than it is to cope with the complications of the present that we have to face. Ignoring reality can sometimes become a bit spooky. There are many who have ended up in hospital because they cannot live in the present at all. Perhaps we should celebrate Halloween, to ensure that we are reminded that living in the past is unhealthy, so we should learn to laugh at it all. Interestingly, the John Gospel tells the beautiful story of Jesus, walking in the Garden of Easter morning and warning Mary Magdalen, "Do not touch me" – and perhaps what the story means is better put,–"do not cling on to the past." It is today that is a gift for us, that is why we call it 'the present!'

All Saints' Day is to remind us of our heritage, but also of our present place among the company of faithful people. We are not in the business of living simply on our own. The lovely words of the Letter to the Hebrews remind us that we are "surrounded by such a great cloud of witnesses." The first saints were martyrs (a word that means witnesses), then confessors and virgins were added to the lists, specially pure or holy people whose example was to be followed, and finally church leaders and bishops were added. The last addition is a pity because it makes it easier for us to imagine that, in order to be a saint, you have to be a vicar! A saint is someone who lives on the intersection between today and tomorrow, between heaven and earth, between life tomorrow and the Kingdom of God.

PSALM

1. "When Israel was only a child, I loved him dearly:
   I called him out of Egypt to become my son.

2. "But the more I called my son, the more he rejected me:
   he worshipped other gods while I was speaking!

3. "Yet I was the parent he knew who taught him to walk:
   it was I who took my own people into my arms,

4. "I always held them close with affection and love:
   when they needed anything, it was I who fed them.

5. "How can I give you up now, my wayward people:
   even if you don't acknowledge me, shall I desert you?

6. "My love for you is stronger than your faith in me:
   even when you reject me I'm at your side.

7. "For I am not merely human, I am your God:
    your holy one who loves you dearly
    is no angry mortal!"

8. Speak to me, my God, as you spoke to Israel:
    you addressed your people of old, so come to us now.

9. For your belief in us is greater than our faith:
    your love for us is deeper than any we know.

10. Help us to know you today as parent of your people:
    I am your adopted child, with my brothers and sisters.

REMEMBRANCE SUNDAY

Addressed to those who fought in the Burma Campaign during World War 2 is the moving epitaph

*"When you go home, tell them of us and say
For your tomorrow we gave our today."*

But it seems so long ago since those battles, let alone those remembering World War 1 with the more familiar words of Lawrence Binyon about remembering the fallen, "at the going down of the sun and in the morning." How long are we to go on remembering?

Perhaps because the 20th century was one of repeated "holocausts" (or "ethnic cleansing"), we are aware of our need to go on remembering, as long as such inhumanities continue. Perhaps because always there are stories of amazing inspiration, that make remembering worth while. There are always people who give their lives, sometimes literally, for others. There's a famous beauty spot in Hawaii, the Pali ridge. People go there for the phenomenal views, to feel the wind in their hair and the exhilaration of the height. But people occasionally go there to commit suicide. One evening, two policemen were beside the fantastic viewpoint, in their car, when one of them noticed a young man preparing to jump. The policeman ran out of the car, and grabbed him. Almost too late. The policeman was himself dragged over the edge. He was saved, with some difficulty, by his partner, who had seen what was happening and had grabbed hold of him. The first policeman was later asked why he hadn't just let go of the young man; after all, there was no point in two people dying, instead of just one, and the young man was nothing to him. But the policeman said there was no way he would have let go, and he would have been quite prepared to die himself as well, if necessary.

Every Step of the Way

Remembering the stories of heroism is what November brings to us each year, with All Saints' Sunday and Remembrance Sunday. For the heroes are a sign for us of God's Kingdom.

In the parish church of Penn, in Buckinghamshire, just behind the pulpit is a little electric switch with a label underneath it. The label says, simply, "Doom." I was reluctant to switch it on, in case the world came to an end! But I was told it was simply to illuminate the old painting of Judgement Day on the wall above. This is the time of year for doom. Like the tramp who once said to me "Remember your end, sir." I first thought he was telling me about a mark on the back of my trousers, so I very nearly replied, "I can't see my end." And that, of course, is true in both senses. Yet we can have some vision of our purpose, our Mission Statement, which the Bible calls the Kingdom of God. The Kingdom Season asks us to remember our end. Remembering those heroes who have gone before us, and looking for what we would really give our lives for.

Someone once said that, when you go to heaven you will simply be told, "Now you can do whatever you really want to do." That is the Kingdom.

PSALM

1. God, we've forgotten your teaching:
   that the kingdom of heaven is close to us!

2. Humanity seems to have been around so long:
   we assume our life just continues forever.

3. We no longer believe in resurrection:
   these days we think we're immortal -

4. progress must continue for humanity:
   even if not for me, the future's infallible.

5. We'd like to believe that life will go on:
   this planet cocooned in the palm of your hand;

6. but isn't that arrogant and selfish:
   where is your promise of the 'end of the world'?

7. A doctor must try to avoid the suggestion of death:
   hospitals are there to keep us alive;

8. surgery can offer me continuing youthfulness:
   any expense is worth while to keep dying at bay.

9. But you have taught us that you are my end:
    it's only by dying that I'm born again;

10. Jesus fulfilled your will by dying:
    to live and settle down was his last temptation.

11. Today we're expected to face global catastrophe:
    the explosion of the earth by volcano or collision,

12. or we'll bomb or pollute ourselves out of existence:
    just like the dinosaurs, humanity could perish.

13. So help me, God, to face up to my end:
    I know I must die, can I find you in my dying?

14. Help us as nations take finality as possible:
    you are in our endings as you were in our beginnings.

15. Guide us in living with the chance of disaster:
    sudden death not the horror that it held
    for our forbears.

16. If you are with me today and close to me this minute:
    your kingdom of heaven is always at hand.

(Published in Psalms of Life)

CHRIST THE KING

The last Sunday of the year is the festival of Christ the King. At the pivotal point of time, when the old (Christian) year gives way to the new one, and the story of Jesus, his birth and life, death and resurrection, begins all over again. The Kingdom season ends with the festival of the King.

"Seek those things that are above, where Christ is..." (Colossians 3.1). It was my school motto, except that we had it in Latin to make it sound better —"Quae sursum sunt quaerite." It is about how we all need to have higher standards in a world which (so often) seems to be going downhill. Everybody should be looking for better things. At my school it was written up on the archway, on the way out to the sports field, because in a boys boarding school the most important activity was what happened on the sports field. At least that was the impression I was given. There was just one thing that troubled me. Up above the archway, where we were being encouraged to raise our sights, was where the maids lived. We all desire higher standards, but somehow it never seems quite so simple!

Every Step of the Way

In St Paul's epistles, there is always a point at which he says, "therefore." Because of all the things he's been writing, "therefore" we must try to live up to these higher standards. As Christ is risen, so we should aim for the things that are above, where Christ is, enthroned as King of the universe. We are encouraged to be "risen with Christ." The "imitation of Christ" (as Thomas a Kempis called it) has always been a powerful image for Christian people, and others. That may be what Paul meant, too. So how do we go about trying to be like Christ? What can mere human beings do in order to get to heaven?

Traditionally, the answer to that has tended to be something like, "be good, and go to church." That is odd, because Jesus did neither, not all the time! He did lots of things people of his day called "bad" – healing people on the Sabbath day, or mixing with bad company. Although he may have attended the synagogue (he certainly never went to "church" by definition!), he tended to be very dismissive of the religious leaders of his day, and in the end the story says they had him put to death. So what can we do in order to get to heaven? The answer is so simple, we don't notice. We are in heaven already. For where God is, there is heaven, and Christ is "with us always, to the end of time." The reason we don't notice is also quite simple. It doesn't always feel like heaven! We are more aware of the times when it does not feel as if God is with us, when things are going wrong, when we are too stressed or fussed, when other people let us down, or we are just plain ill or hurt, for accidents will happen. So we easily begin to think that God is not with us at all. If only Christian people were able to be true to the faith they profess! God is perhaps closest to us when things are bad.

Footprints is about a dream. There are two sets of footprints in the sand, when I am feeling lonely and by myself. That's all right, God says to us, I am always walking along beside you, no matter what happens, I am with you always. But then, we notice that, at times when things are really bad there seems to be only one set of footprints in the sand, where had God gone to then? "Ah that," God says, "is when I was carrying you."

A human being is in heaven, Christ is the King. And heaven is for us, too. Not just after we are dead, when we have "gone to be with Jesus." That is, as we all know, a childish view, even if there is an element of comfort in it. For God is with us always, even today. God does not wait for us to be good (God help us all, if he did!). God does not wait for you to go to church (God help most of the world, if he did that, too!). Nor does God wait for you to be dead! God is with you day by day. That is what the festival of Christ the King means.

At the coronation of a king or queen in Britain, the new monarch is given the orb to hold. The explanation for the orb is that it is the world set under the cross, since the whole world is under the kingship of the crucified Jesus who is King of all. Christ is king of kings, even. The danger of our world is that Christians seem often to give the impression that Jesus is my personal saviour, and no more. He stands over our public life, too, in judgement against the domination of the rich or the powerful. But how can we point to this rule of Christ in our own work and home and life with others? We have tended to say that we can do that by keeping my own hands clean, by looking for higher personal standards for myself, and by keeping my head down. Nobody wants a Jesus freak pointing out their sins to them every five minutes! But that is wrong.

We are here to affirm other people, not stand over them in judgement. To remember that God is with us always, in all of our lives. For God's Kingdom is here. Christ is King. He is with us every day, no matter what may happen.

PSALM

1. You, God, are ruler of heaven and earth:
    you have exalted your Son to his rightful Kingdom.

2. Risen and ascended he is Lord of the universe:
    you have given him authority as Christ the King.

3. Now his rule has exploded into all the world:
    he is with us for all time and in all places.

4. As a human being he was born and died:
    now humanity is risen and glorified.

5. We can be confident in your power to save us:
    since through your Spirit we have known his glory.

6. For all the earth is yours:
    giving power to our King, you give us courage also.

7. With him we too can be exalted:
    we can share a part in his Kingdom
    while living our life on earth.

125

Every Step of the Way

ABOUT PARISH AND PEOPLE

PARISH AND PEOPLE was founded in 1949 and was instrumental in effecting a quiet revolution in popularising the parish communion. In 1963 it merged with the Keble Conference Group to spearhead movements towards team ministry, synodical government and church unity. In 1970 it was largely responsible for the formation of the ecumenical movement 'ONE for Christian Renewal'.

PARISH AND PEOPLE has, however, continued to promote new life in the Anglican denomination, and publishes a range of stimulating material for parishes and deaneries in order to enable the growth from the grass roots up of a lively open people's church in which lay ministry can blossom.

THE DEANERY RESOURCE UNIT was launched in 1989, over 250 deaneries throughout the Church of England subscribing to this bi-annual mailing, which includes the well-established Deanery Exchange leaflet and 'Starter', together booklets and briefings on matters of deanery concern. (Selected titles given below). The Unit is working in collaboration with the Church House Deaneries Group to bring a breath of fresh air to the 'missing link' in the C of E's structure. Your ideas for future developments are most welcome.

DRU MAILING £12 a year single subscription (50 copies of DX); £20 double (100 copies of DX) Starter Pack £5 - includes Deanery Exchange and a selection of briefings and booklets.

Booklets   (£2 each)
The Rise of the Deanery
Chairing the Synod
Making the Deanery Work
Leading the Deanery
Flying Deanery Kites
Deaneries, Evangelism and Unity
Devolution to the Deanery
Ministry in the Deanery
Devolution 2, Loosing the Apron Strings
A Look at Rural Deans and Deaneries
Training for Local Ministry
Pastoral Reorganisation
Communications in the Deanery
All Together Now
Consultation & Training for Rural Deans

Conference Reports (£2 each)
A Bridge Thus Far (1998)
Catching The New Vision (2000)
Like It Or Lump It (2002)

Briefings (£1 each)
The Role of the Rural Dean
Deanery Mission Audit
Guidelines for Deanery Officers
Training for the Lay Chair
Setting the Agenda
The Deanery and Ecumenism
Pastoral Committees
Church House Deaneries Group
Money Matters
The Deanery Specialist
This is your Synod

Specials (£2 each)
Psalms of Life
Psalms for the Synod
The Parish Magazine Inset
Victorian Church News
Daybreak (£5.00)